WALKS FOR ALL AGES
STAFFORDSHIRE

WALKS FOR ALL AGES

STAFFORDSHIRE

HUGH TAYLOR & MOIRA McCROSSAN

BRADWELL
BOOKS

Published by Bradwell Books
9 Orgreave Close Sheffield S13 9NP
Email: books@bradwellbooks.co.uk

British Library Cataloguing in Publication Data: a catalogue record for this book is available from the British Library.

1st Edition

ISBN: 9781909914827

Print: Gomer Press, Llandysul, Ceredigion SA44 4JL

Design by: Erik Siewko Creative, Derbyshire.
eriksiewko@gmail.com

Photograph Credits: © Hugh Taylor & Moira McCrossan
and credited seperately where applicable.

Maps: Contain Ordnance Survey data
© Crown copyright and database right 2015

Ordnance Survey licence number 100039353

The information in this book has been produced in good faith and is intended as a general guide. Bradwell Books and its authors have made all reasonable efforts to ensure that the details are correct at the time of publication. Bradwell Books and the author cannot accept any responsibility for any changes that have taken place subsequent to the book being published. It is the responsibility of individuals undertaking any of the walks listed in this publication to exercise due care and consideration for the health and wellbeing of each other in the party. Particular care should be taken if you are inexperienced. The walks in this book are not especially strenuous but individuals taking part should ensure they are fit and able to complete the walk before setting off.

WALKS FOR ALL AGES

Walk 1.	Abbots Bromley	2½ miles	p. 8
Walk 2.	Essington	2½ miles	p. 12
Walk 3.	Whittington	2 miles	p. 16
Walk 4.	Chasewater	3¼ miles	p. 20
Walk 5.	Middleton Lakes	3 miles	p. 24
Walk 6.	Tutbury	2 miles	p. 28
Walk 7.	Burton upon Trent	2½ miles	p. 32
Walk 8.	Longnor	2¼ miles	p. 36
Walk 9.	Tittesworth Reservoir	4½ miles	p. 40
Walk 10.	Lud's Church	2 miles	p. 44
Walk 11.	Wetton	3 miles	p. 48
Walk 12.	Barlaston	3 miles	p. 52
Walk 13.	Milwich	3 miles	p. 56
Walk 14.	Great Haywood	4 miles	p. 60
Walk 15.	Etruria	3½ miles	p. 64
Walk 16.	Cheddleton	2 miles	p. 70
Walk 17.	Trysull	2¼ miles	p. 76
Walk 18.	Cannock Chase	3 miles	p. 80
Walk 19.	Lichfield	2½ miles	p. 84
Walk 20.	Alrewas	3 miles	p. 90

INTRODUCTION

WALKING IN STAFFORDSHIRE, YOU WILL FIND THE REMAINS OF IRON AGE FORTS, VILLAGES DATING BACK TO THE DOMESDAY BOOK, WILD WOODLAND, MEDIEVAL CASTLES AND A CATHEDRAL WITH THREE SPIRES.

The Victorians and their immediate predecessors left the mark of the Industrial Revolution on the countryside, although the belching chimneys, grinding mills and coal seams have given way to industrial museums, wildlife parks and walks along disused railway lines. Above all, this county is criss-crossed by canals, combining industrial heritage with beautiful and peaceful countryside.

At the start of the Industrial Revolution in the Potteries, the canals were crucial. Along with James Brindley, a pioneering canal builder, Josiah Wedgwood was one of the prime movers in growing the canal network. The stories of their lives and achievements can be discovered as you follow various walks in this book. Look for Brindley's Bratch Locks at Trysull and his statue at Etruria. Wedgwood's story is also told at Etruria and Barlaston.

The history is fascinating but the canals have now become beautiful and lively places, teeming with wildlife. It is a delight to walk here or simply sit at one of the many canalside inns, watching the boats. Many of the industrial sites have been transformed into wildlife areas, with old quarries flooded to attract birds and reservoirs transformed to encourage wildlife and provide facilities for watersports.

Beyond the canals and industrial heritage, wherever you walk, you can find pretty villages like Milwich, Abbots Bromley or Longnor. Wander through Milwich's interesting graveyard or look in the church at Abbots Bromley for the horns used in the ancient Horn Dance; or better still visit in September to see it performed. At Longnor you can wander through the central market square to find the 'Table of Tolls' still displayed on the old Market Hall.

You can also walk through some amazing natural formations, around which tales have been woven. Lud's Church at Meerbrook is a natural chasm, created by landslips, where an ancient poem tells us Sir Gawain confronted the Green Knight. Have a look too at the magnificent Thor's Cave, at Wetton, where Ken Russell set the story of the White Worm in his 1988 film.

You will never tire of walking in Staffordshire, a county where the signs of human habitation stretch back into the mists of time and the landscape, both natural and shaped by its people, is fascinating and beautiful.

© Stephen Jones

ABBOTS BROMLEY

Walk round this sleepy little village, which comes magically alive for one day each September as the villagers re-enact the centuries-old Horn Dance.

The famous Horn Dance is an unbroken Folk Dance tradition dating from the Middle Ages. Although there are no written records of it earlier than the 16th century, the antlers that are in use today are reindeer antlers that were carbon dated and confirmed as being from the 11th century.

The dance always takes place on Wakes Monday, the day after Wakes Sunday, a moveable feast, which is the first Sunday after 4 September. It's a long day, starting at 7.45 am with a special service in the village church, where the sets of horns are kept in special holders fastened to one of the walls. The church is normally open to visitors so you can see them. They are very heavy, so imagine how tired the dancers are at the end of the day, when they return to the church, having covered about ten miles round the district and performed the dance at many locations, including several pubs and Blithfield Hall, home of Lady Bagot.

The dance troupe has twelve members, all male. Six of them carry the antlers and are supported by traditional characters, Maid Marian (played by a man), The Hobby Horse and the archer plus two musicians and a triangle player.

The first time we saw it we talked to Doug Fowell, accordion player and senior member. The Fowells have been the leading family in the dance for several generations. Doug started on the triangle when he was seven, became the leading musician in 1948 and participated in his last dance two months before he died in 2006, a total of 71 performances. Abbots Bromley is normally a sleepy little village but on Dance Day it is transformed. Visitors come from all over to watch, participate and follow the dance. Visiting Morris sides take turns to dance in the streets and there are various other stalls and entertainments laid on for those who don't want to go traipsing across the countryside following the dancers.

Eventually, though, the dance returns to Abbots Bromley and following the last performances outside the Coach and Horses in the High Street and the Village Green, where they first danced many hours earlier, they return to the church at 8.15pm and the horns get put back in their mounts for another year.

THE BASICS

Distance: 2½ miles / 4km

Gradient: Slight

Severity: Easy

Approx. time to walk: 1½ hours

Stiles: Six

Map: OS Explorer 244 (Cannock Chase and Chasewater)

Path description: Mainly footpaths through fields. Some country lanes and pavement in the village

Start point: The Old Buttermarket (GR SK 080245)

Parking: On the village street near the Buttermarket (WS15 3BS)

Dog friendly: Only if your dog can cope with the stiles

Public toilets: None on the route. Nearest at Rugeley Library, Anson Street

Nearest food: The Crown Hotel at the start

ABBOTS BROMLEY WALK

1. Head along the High Street with the Buttermarket behind you. When you reach the Coach and Horses turn left into Radmore Lane.

2. Just before the end of the 30mph limit, turn left through a gate and onto a footpath running between two tennis courts. At the end of the courts turn right onto a paved track, then almost immediately veer off it onto a track that leads onto the village cricket green. Go round the perimeter of the green to reach a kissing gate in the far right corner.

3. Go through the gate onto Swan Lane but turn immediately right onto the Staffordshire Way. Go through another kissing gate then veer 45 degrees left and follow a faint footpath downhill towards a gap in some trees. Go through this then keep downhill, aiming for a kissing gate about halfway along the far hedge. Go through this to cross a wooden footbridge then cross a stile and follow the footpath in the same direction to cross a stile into the next field. Then head uphill and over the next stile. Head uphill again from here towards a hedgerow. In the corner of the next field cross a stile by a water trough then turn immediately right to go over another stile, cross this field then cross a final stile on this stretch to get onto a track and proceed to a T-junction with a lane.

4. Turn left and walk along this lane as it turns left then heads first downhill, then climbs to enter the village at School Lane.

5. At the bottom of School Lane turn left to pass by The Crown. Cross High Street and turn left, then right into Hall Hill Lane. Head up

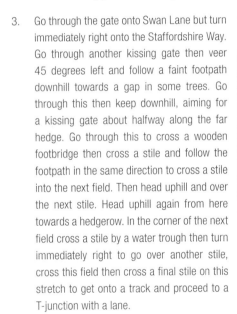

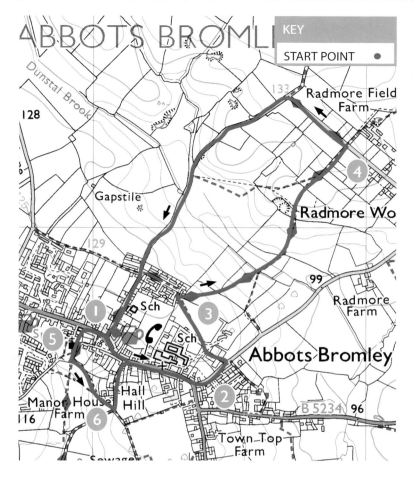

here to go through a gate by a cattle grid, pass by some farm buildings and proceed along a track.

6.   When you come to a junction turning right, cross a stile just before it then veer right to pass to the left of a barn then head towards the tower of the church. Cross a stile into the churchyard and follow the path to the front door. Head inside and have a look around. You'll see the reindeer antlers the dancers carry for miles each year for the Horn Dance. In a glass case nearby you'll see the hat of the wonderful Doug Fowell. Leave the church and head along the street then turn right to get back to the start.

ESSINGTON

A PLEASANT FLAT WALK ALONG FOOTPATHS AND AN OLD
RAILWAY LINE, IN THE FOOTSTEPS OF A LONG-DEAD KING.
THIS IS DEFINITELY ONE WALK WHERE YOU WANT A POCKET
FIELD GUIDE TO BIRDS BECAUSE IT'S ONE OF THE PRIME
LOCATIONS FOR TWITCHERS IN THE AREA.

At Essington Quarry Pool and in the woods you can see an amazing variety of birdlife including wags, tits, heron, woodpeckers, goldcrest and nuthatches. There are varieties of duck, grebe, willow warblers, yellowhammers and robin redbreasts. Depending on the time of year you visit, you may see swallows, skylarks and swifts, pheasants, reed bunting, pigeons, blackbirds, magpies and coots. And it's not beyond the bounds of possibility to spot the odd black-backed gull or arctic tern.

The Monarch's Way is a 615-mile (990km) walking trail that follows the escape of Charles II after the Battle of Worcester in 1651. It's easily recognised by its distinctive way-markers, a yellow disk with a black royal oak tree with a yellow feathered crown of the Prince of Wales and above it the ship, The Surprise. The trail starts at Worcester and ends in Brighton after going through Bristol and Yeovil.

The Wulfrun Way is a walking path just 15 miles (24km) long that runs along the outskirts of Wolverhampton and Chasewater, using the trackbeds of redundant colliery railways and canal towpaths. It owes its name to an Anglo-Saxon noblewoman of the 10th and 11th centuries. She founded an estate near Wolverhampton in 985 and a convent at Tamworth where she may be buried. There's a statue of her in front of St Peter's Church in Wolverhampton and her name appears frequently on buildings and businesses, notably the Wulfrun Centre and the Wulfrun Hotel.

The motte that you pass on this walk was allegedly the home of Ealhswith, a princess of the 9th century. She was the daughter of a Mercian nobleman but thought to be descended from Mercian royalty through her mother. In 868, she married Alfred the Great, famous for allegedly burning an old woman's cakes. Alfred succeeded his brother as King of Wessex in 871. It was he who started using the title King of the Anglo-Saxons.

Alfred died in 899 and their son, Edward the Elder, became King of the Anglo-Saxons and had his court at Winchester. When his mother died in 902 she was buried in the New Minster at Winchester.

THE BASICS

Diistance: 2½ miles / 4 km

Gradient: Mostly flat

Severity: Easy

Approx time to walk: 1½ to 2 hours

Stiles: None

Maps: OS Explorer 219 (Wolverhampton and Dudley)

Path description: Field footpaths, old railway trackbed & short sections of road

Start Point: Old railway on B4156, west of Essington (GR SJ 948024)

Parking: Small parking space in front of the gates onto the old railway trackbed on Blackhalve Lane (B4156) between Essington and Wednesfield (WV11 2BB)

Dog friendly: Yes

Public toilets: None on the route

Nearest food: Wednesfield has a selection of eating places. But this is the perfect walk for a picnic

ESSINGTON WALK

1. From the roadside, walk past the barrier and along the old railway trackbed. Keep a look out for a footpath on the right that goes through a gate in the fence with two wooden gateposts. Go onto this footpath and follow it along the edge of some fields. This is the Monarch's Way.

2. When you reach another path heading off to the left go along it for the best views of Essington Quarry Pool. This is a favourite haunt of local birdwatchers and it is not unusual to come across several twitchers armed with binoculars, spotting scopes and cameras. There's a bench conveniently situated along here; just the spot for a picnic lunch. When you are done here re-trace your steps to the Monarch's Way and turn left.

3. At the next junction of paths turn right and walk along the edge of a field. Go through another gap in the hedge onto a track. This is part of the Wulfrun Way. Keep right and follow this path into woodland and across a stile. There are several paths going through the wood. Do your best to keep straight ahead to reach the corner of the wood, where you will find a stile with a Wulfrun Way marker pole. Turn right here and head down the other edge of the wood and out onto the fields.

4. Continue heading south on a path between two fields. When you pass what looks like a clump of trees stop and have a look around. This is an ancient motte. In the summer nettles and the undergrowth will probably prevent you from exploring it further. Local legend has this lost settlement as the home

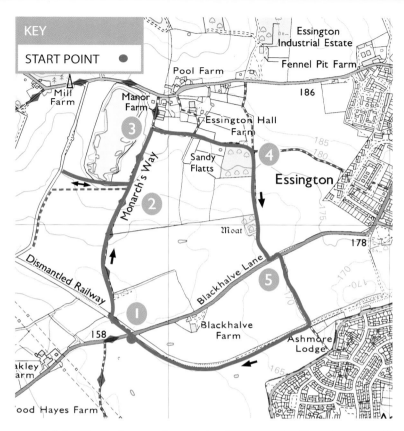

KEY

START POINT ●

of Ealhswith. Continue on the path to pass another barrier and go onto a road.

5. Carefully cross the road and turn left. In a few hundred yards turn right onto a footpath and make your way along it, passing several fields. Then go down some steps and turn right onto the bed of an old railway track. Follow this back to the start.

WHITTINGTON

A PRETTY, UNPRETENTIOUS LITTLE VILLAGE WHERE THE COVENTRY CANAL MEETS THE BIRMINGHAM AND FAZELEY CANAL.

Initially the Coventry Canal was to have been constructed to run from Coventry to link into the Trent and Mersey Canal at Fradley, and work was authorised under a 1768 Act of Parliament. By 1771 it had reached Atherstone, but with about ten miles to go the company ran out of money and all work stopped. In 1784, after overcoming significant opposition from other canal companies, the Birmingham and Fazeley Canal Company received authorisation to proceed with their plan to provide a shorter link with London. To make this work they needed the Coventry Canal completed to Fradley. Negotiations took place amongst several companies and agreement was reached that would create a much wider network. As a result the Coventry Canal Company built the short section to Fazeley and the Birmingham and Fazeley Company created the stretch to Whittington Brook. It opened in 1790.

Whittington has existed since the 12th century, but people have lived here much longer, possibly as far back as the Iron Age. There has been a church here since the 13th century. It's dedicated to St Giles, the patron saint of beggars and lepers. The church was almost totally destroyed by fire in 1761 with only parts of the tower surviving, most of which has been incorporated in the present building. Three of the original bells also survived and continued to be rung until the wooden beams supporting them rotted and they were removed in 1990 to be replaced by a peal of six late Victorian Bells from St James's Church in Islington. The frame that was built then was designed to hang eight bells and a further two were finally added in 2008.

In the churchyard you will find a simple memorial in the shape of a stone cross marking the grave of Thomas Spencer. He farmed at High Hill Farm from 1903 until his death in 1905 at the relatively young age of 53. He is better remembered for the £300 investment he made, starting up a business with Michael Marks in 1894. Marks and Spencer is still a household name. Spencer took the fortune he had made in a few short years and used it to buy his farm. The Thomas Spencer Hall in Church Street is named after him and was partly financed by his donation.

THE BASICS

Distance: 2 miles / 3.2km

Gradient: Flat

Severity: Easy

Approx. time to walk: 1¼ to 1½ hours

Stiles: Two

Map: OS Explorer 232 (Nuneaton and Tamworth)

Path description: Canal towpaths, well-surfaced tracks and pavement, one slightly muddy footpath

Start point: Site of the former Old Swan Inn (now demolished) on Burton Road in Whittington (GR SK 162088)

Parking: On Burton Road near Swan Cottages just before the canal bridge (WS14 9PH)

Dog friendly: Mainly dog friendly; they can squeeze through the stiles

Public toilets: No public toilets

Nearest food: The Dog Inn on the walk

WHITTINGTON WALK

1. Head down Burton Road towards the canal bridge. Pass Swan Cottages on the right just before the bridge then cross the bridge, turn right down some steps and head along the canal towpath. Keep a look out for the stone and plaque marking the spot where the Coventry Canal meets the Birmingham to Fazeley. When you reach Whittington Bridge go left through a gate and uphill to the road.

2. Turn right to cross the bridge then cross the road. Turn left at a footpath sign onto a broad track and follow it to reach a white farmhouse. Turn right here then right again onto Vicarage Lane.

3. Keep on this well-surfaced lane, passing the local cricket ground on your left, a park on your right then finally exiting onto the main road by a hospice. Cross the road then turn left and continue to reach the corner of Fishwick Road and Main Street, by the Dog Inn.

4. Turn right into Main Street, cross the road and head along, passing Chapel Lane on your left, then turn left just before the local Cooperative shop onto Blacksmith Lane. At its end cross the road and continue down a narrow footpath. This can be muddy during rainy periods. At the footpath's end cross the first stile on the route. There should be enough room for a dog to get through, then turn right along another footpath along the edge of a field to cross another stile. This passes some allotments then turns right onto a residential street.

5. From here follow the road through this housing estate to the junction of Neal Croft and Burton Road. Turn either right or left here depending on where you managed to park.

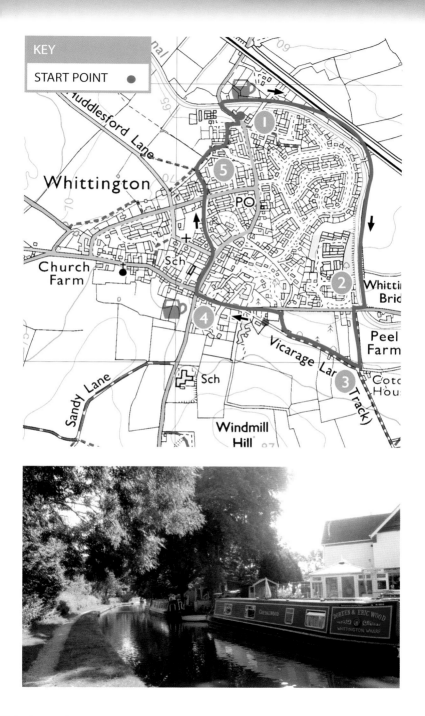

KEY

START POINT ●

Huddlesford Lane

Whittington

P O

Church
Farm

Sch

Whittin
Brid

Peel
Farm

Vicarage Lar

Sandy Lane

Sch

Cota
Hou

Windmill
Hill

CHASEWATER

A WATERSIDE WALK ON WELL-SURFACED PATHS WITH A
HERITAGE RAILWAY AND LOTS OF WATER SPORTS AND
CHILDREN'S ACTIVITIES THROWN IN FOR GOOD MEASURE.

The reservoir here was created in 1797 by building two dams to increase the water levels in Norton Pool. It was used to keep the water levels on the Birmingham Canal Network at a constant level and provide a direct feed to the Wyrley and Essington Canal. Surplus water from the canals was then returned to the reservoir using a steam-driven pump.

From the middle of the 19th century the coal seams round the reservoir and even under it were opened and a rail network was created linking the various mines to the reservoir. But the coming of the railway meant less traffic on the canals and by the mid-1950s several branches of the original canal had closed with a consequent drop in the need for water from the reservoir.

When it was sold in 1956 to the local council, Norton Pool was renamed Chasewater. By this time most of the mines were closing and the railways, no longer needed to move coal, were abandoned, leaving a desolate industrial wasteland. The transformation was swift as sailing dinghies and then speedboats appeared and a sailing club was formed. By 1961 there was a funfair, followed by a pier and a castle, while rail and canal traffic had ceased. Towards the end of the 20th century Chasewater became a country park much frequented by sailors, water skiers, anglers and even twitchers.

On this walk you will encounter the Chasewater Railway at several points. This popular heritage railway, operating on the tracks of the former colliery railway, has a variety of steam and diesel locomotives pulling vintage carriages along the nearly four miles of track that run round the reservoir. There are four stations or stops. Brownhills West, the western terminus and headquarters, is built in Victorian style. It was constructed here after the original station had to be moved because of the construction of the M6 Toll motorway.

It has a heritage centre and museum, with displays of railway and mining artefacts as well as vintage carriages and engines. The other stops are Chasetown, the north-eastern terminus, which has no facilities, Norton Lakeside Halt, which is similar but is a great starting point for walkers and cyclists, and Chasewater Heaths Station, which has a buffet and shop.

THE BASICS

Distance: 3¼ miles / 5.2km

Gradient: Flat

Severity: Easy

Approx. time to walk: 2 hours

Stiles: None

Map: OS Explorer 244 (Cannock Chase and Chasewater)

Path description: Gravel and metalled tracks, lanes and footpaths

Start point: Chasewater Country Park (GR SK 040078)

Parking: On the roadside at the start (nearest postcode WS7 3QW)

Dog friendly: This is a very popular dog walk

Public toilets: South Shore Cafe

Nearest food. South Shore Cafe on the route

1. From the start point go through a gate onto a well-surfaced path. Keep on this path, ignoring turns to the left until it reaches the main road, then veers left, go left and head uphill to go through another gate. Eventually it will head downhill through a wooded area to reach a T-junction near a fingerpost.

2. Go right here then keep on, ignoring junctions until you come to another T-junction. Turn left here and keep going to reach the level crossing gates, signal box and buildings at Chasewater Heaths Station.

3. Go through a kissing gate onto a broad gravel path and head over heathland. Look out for deer grazing. Ignore a footpath sign and eventually reach another kissing gate, go through it then eventually go up an incline and turn left onto a path by the railway.

4. This is Norton Lakeside Halt. Walk along beside the platform then the track on a narrow path, which once again reaches a broad track. Follow this along the edge of the lake for some distance to reach Brownhills West Station.

5. From here keep to the lakeside path that meanders round the edge of the water. This is very popular with families and has lots of facilities including boat hire, mini golf and the spectacular and adventurous Cable Wakeboarding where a zip wire pulls water boarders along and over ramps and jumps.

6. After the pier turn left and walk along the lake then onto the end of Pool Lane. Turn left to return to the start.

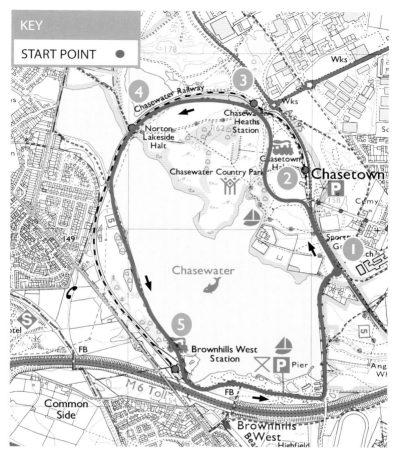

KEY

START POINT •

THIS PARTICULARLY FINE WALK AROUND AN RSPB NATURE RESERVE IS PERFECT FOR THE SERIOUS BIRDWATCHER BUT ALSO A GREAT PLACE TO INTRODUCE CHILDREN TO BIRDWATCHING AND NATURE. SMALL CHILDREN WILL LOVE THE PLAY MEADOW, WHERE THEY CAN EXPLORE A MAZE, TRY POND DIPPING AND ON OCCASION LEARN ABOUT DEN BUILDING.

Just a few years ago Middleton Lakes was a commercial gravel quarry. Then in 2007 the RSPB acquired it and developed it into this reserve. They altered the gravel pits then flooded them to create the lakes and habitat for the many bird species that now live or visit here. The Birmingham and Fazeley Canal runs through the reserve and you will cross it on the walk. As well as the lakes there are meadows and ancient woodlands that attract non-aquatic birds.

Heron Count

Check here for updates on how many pairs, nests + chicks there are in the heronry.

Currently there are....

28 Active nests, 20 of them have chicks.

There are 38 chicks of varying ages.

The 1st Chicks fledged on the 21st April

What you see is dependent on when you visit. The reserve attracts a large number of wildfowl species in the winter including smews, pochards and tufted ducks. Look out for bitterns in the fringes of the reed-beds and lesser spotted woodpeckers and willow tits around the feeders. Harriers, peregrines and merlins hang almost motionless in the air, ready to plummet earthwards onto their prey.

Spring is when the reserve really starts to move up a gear as migrating birds go through mating rituals and nest building. The heronry has been active with up to twenty breeding pairs of grey herons, and as the young leave the nests you can see up to a hundred birds in the sky. The call of the cuckoo, the song of the skylark and the profusion of bluebells and other wild flowers leaves no doubt that spring has arrived.

Summer is the best time to spot long-tailed tits, swallows and swifts, when the place is teeming with the insects they feed on.

The pools are alive with dragonflies but the meadows are the best place to see cinnabar and burnet moths. On sunny days you might even see a grass snake enjoying the heat. In the evenings the owls and bats swoop in pursuit of their supper.

Herons stalk the lakes in the autumn ready to spear fish, and kingfishers dart past in a blur of blue. Various fungi will be growing in the woods and the fair-weather birds will be starting their long journey south to warmer climes as in turn the over-wintering birds return.

THE BASICS

Distance: 3 miles / 4.8km

Gradient: Flat

Severity: Easy

Approx. time to walk: 1½ to 2 hours

Stiles: None

Map: OS Explorer 232 (Nuneaton and Tamworth)

Path description: Well-surfaced and dirt footpaths

Start point: Middleton Lakes reserve car park, behind Middleton Hall (GR SP 194983)

Parking: RSPB Reserve Car Park (charge) (B78 2AE)

Dog friendly: No: there are lots of parts of this reserve where dogs are not permitted

Public toilets: At the Welcome Barn

Nearest food: Café at Middleton Hall

MIDDLETON LAKES WALK

1. From the end of the car park follow the fingerpost pointing to Woodland, Wetland and Meadow Trails. Go through a kissing gate and carefully cross the road and go onto a wooden walkway on the other side. Along this walkway are lots of interpretation boards telling you about the herons that nest here from January to July. When you come off the walkway, continue following the signs for the Wetland Trail. Soon you will see signs telling you to keep your dog on a lead at all times and pointing out that there are some parts of the reserve not open to dogs. This walk goes through some of these parts.

2. Soon you will reach a viewing point on the right. It has benches, and if you sit here very quietly you never know what you may see. When you have seen enough continue along the trail. When you come across a fingerpost pointing left into the wood follow it, heading towards the Wetlands Trail. Cross a wooden bridge then a wooden walkway. Just to the right of the walkway is a bench and a sign telling you that this is a good place to spot a kingfisher, but only if you are really quiet. The next sign tells you to look out for nesting boxes and how to spot them. Finally cross another wooden bridge and the path swings left. Shortly

after that the Woodland Trail ends in a junction by a fingerpost. Take the right turn to follow the Wetland and Meadow Trails. When the path reaches Fisher's Mill Bridge, the trails part.

3. Cross the bridge and at a fingerpost turn left onto the Wetland Trail. Soon you will encounter your first sign telling you that dogs are not allowed on this part of the reserve. It explains that the very smell of a dog may prevent otters from breeding in the area. So if you have a dog, turn back. Otherwise continue following the

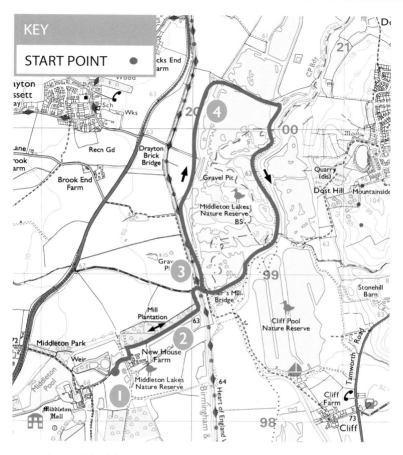

path round the lakes to reach the Jubilee hide. See if you can spot lapwings, redshanks, oystercatchers and ringed plovers. You might even see a heron.

4. From the hide turn left and continue along the west side of the lake. Eventually you will reach a gate and a fingerpost indicating a right turn. Take it and at the next junction you can turn left to head up to another hide or turn right to go down the east side of the lake. It is impossible to get lost on this walk. Keep ahead following the fingerposts and eventually you will return to Fisher's Mill Bridge. Then simply re-trace your steps along the Woodland Trail to return to the car park. If you want a longer walk then turn left at Fisher's Mill Bridge to complete the circuit of the Meadow Walks.

TUTBURY

A SPLENDID RIVER WALK WITH A GENTLE STROLL THROUGH A QUAINT AND HISTORIC TOWN COMPLETE WITH A RUINED MEDIEVAL CASTLE AND ITS RESIDENT GHOSTS.

Tutbury started life as a fortified village in Saxon Mercia. It was one of only three burghs in the country at the time of the Domesday Book. It was once famous for Tutbury Crystal and until 2006 it was possible to visit their premises and watch the craftsmen at work. Then they moved the entire operation to Stoke-on-Trent, but the move was unsuccessful and the company that bought them out now again operates a showroom in Tutbury. But the glass is manufactured elsewhere.

There are a number of listed buildings in the town, the most attractive being its Norman Church, St Mary's Priory Church. The west front of the present building dates to the 12th century with most of the rest being 13th century in origin. The south tower was added in the 16th century, the north aisle in the early 19th century and the chancel and sanctuary were renewed in 1866.

Tutbury Castle is allegedly one of the most haunted castles in England. Amongst the spectral inhabitants are a soldier, the almost obligatory White Lady and Mary, Queen of Scots. Mary is one of the great tragic figures of history. The daughter of King James V of Scotland, she was just six days old when her father died. Until she was of an age to rule, Scotland was governed by regents, while she was brought up in France. More French than Scottish, she was married to the French Dauphin when she was just sixteen and was briefly Queen of France until her husband died in December 1560. The following August she arrived in Scotland, but after a stormy six years and defeat in battle by the Protestant lords, she abdicated in 1567. She spent most of the rest of her short life as a prisoner of Elizabeth I, before being beheaded at the age of forty-four at Fotheringhay Castle in Northamptonshire.

It was in January 1569 that responsibility for her custody was entrusted to the Earl of Shrewsbury and his wife Bess of Hardwick. Apparently Mary did not like her new home and complained about the damp and draughts. For many years the castle organized popular ghost hunts. The last was in March 2015, but they have been replaced by torchlight tours and atmospheric historical performances.

THE BASICS

Distance: 3 miles / 6km
Gradient: Some inclines and steps
Severity: Moderate
Time: 1½ hrs
Stiles: None
Map: OS Explorer 219 (Wolverhampton & Dudley)
Path description: Gravel and earth
Start point: Moorcroft Environment Centre (GR SO 969950)
Parking: On street and is close to bus routes (WS10 8GA)
Dogs: Allowed but site rules need to be adhered to
Toilets: None
Refreshments: None

TUTBURY WALK

1. Leave the car park and cross to the Leopard. Turn left then right into Castle Street. Head uphill on the pavement ignoring the right turn signed for the castle. You can visit it after the walk.

2. Near the top of the hill where the road starts to curve left and Castle Street runs into Park Lane, turn right by a public footpath sign and onto a narrow footpath to the right of a house. Follow this downhill to go through a kissing gate and into a field. From the top of the footpath you will have seen the line of the path stretching out before you. Follow it, veering slightly right, to the end of the first field, go over a stile and continue to the next. Go over a stile, cross a footbridge and over another stile. There are wide gaps in the stiles and dogs should manage them without any bother.

3. You are now on a Duchy of Lancaster permissive footpath. Keep ahead across this field, through a section of fence and across the weir to arrive on the riverbank of the Dove. This is a popular spot with local families so don't be surprised if it is busy.

4. Continue from the weir following the bank of the river on a well-trodden path. Keep to the right of the fence otherwise you might have difficulties later when the other path by the river peters out. Follow the course of the river, with great views of the castle to your right, all the way round to reach a high banking.

5. Climb this and drop down onto a track, which leads past the cricket green. Go through a kissing gate then veer right through Tutbury Mill Park, the site of a former gypsum mill. Look out for a large gypsum boulder and a set of mill wheels. Go across a white bridge and exit onto the road. Turn right onto Bridge Street.

6. Continue along here to the junction with Monk Street. Keep ahead past Tutbury Mill Mews. At the next junction turn right into Castle Street. You'll pass the local museum, which is worth a visit and is free. Shortly after that the car park is on your right.

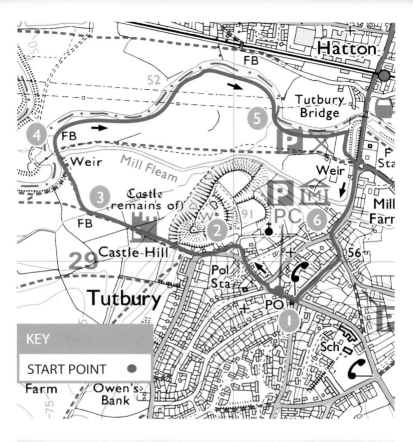

KEY

START POINT ●

BURTON UPON TRENT

BEER, BREWING AND THE TRENT WASHLANDS ARE ALL ON
THE MENU OF THIS TOWN AND COUNTRY WALK.

St Modwen, an Irish noblewoman of the 7th
century, stopped here for several years on her
pilgrimage to Rome and had a little chapel built
on an island in the river. When she returned from
Rome she built another church and dedicated it
to St Peter. Later in the early 11th century the
Saxon Earl Wulfric Spot founded a Benedictine
abbey on the ground that is now partly covered
by the Market Hall. Staffordshire was a rebellious
place and apparently William the Conqueror had
to visit twice to put down insurrections. He took
the opportunity while here to visit the abbey and
the shrine of Saint Modwen. Burton is recorded
in the Domesday Book of 1086 but unfortunately
misnamed as Stafford.

The bulk of this walk is close to the banks of the
River Trent and through the floodplain between
St Peter's and Burton Bridges. This area was subject to frequent flooding, which fertilised
and enriched the soil, producing first-class grazing. In the 14th century the monks of
Burton Abbey increased their sheep flocks and became important wool traders. The wells
in the Washlands produced water that had been hardened by gypsum. This, as the monks
discovered, is very good for brewing beer and is one of the factors that has made the town
a major brewing centre.

The brewing industry first started by the medieval monks expanded and by the 19th
century it was the main industry. At its peak in 1881, it was producing 25 per cent
of all beer brewed in Britain and exporting it all over the world. The brewing families
controlled the town council and even supplied the Members of Parliament. Although
the families have gone, their names live on as brands such as Bass, Worthington and
Marston. Nowadays the big players are Coors, who produce Worthington and Carling, and
Marston's, who produce Marston's, Hobgoblin and also draught Bass under a licensing
agreement. However, there are also a number of microbreweries supplying local pubs.

An interesting spin-off from the brewery industry was the invention of Marmite, made from brewer's yeast. The Marmite Food Extract Company was formed here in Burton in 1902 and it's still made in the town. After your walk you can find out more of the history of brewing by heading to the National Brewery Centre.

THE BASICS

Distance: 2½ miles / 4km

Gradient: Mostly flat

Severity: Easy

Approx. time to walk: 1½ to 2 hours

Stiles: None

Map: OS Explorer 245 (The National Forest)

Path description: Mainly well-surfaced footpaths and pavement

Start point: Fleet Street car park, Burton (GR SK 249224)

Parking: Fleet Street car park, Burton (charge) (DE14 3RZ)

Dog friendly: Very

Public toilets: In Market Place, town centre, on the walk

Nearest food: Lots of options around Market Place

BURTON UPON TRENT WALK

1. Exit the car park and head towards a cycle route sign for Stapenhill. Go onto the Stapenhill Viaduct, which was given to the town in 1889 by the brewer Baron of Burton. A short way along this is a ramp leading to the left. Go down it then turn right onto a footpath.

2. Follow this path, keeping left where it forks then turning left over a footbridge. Follow the Washlands signpost for the town centre. When you reach a block of stone with a plaque for the Land and Water sculpture by Rosemary Terry, turn right and go into a clearing in some trees to view the artwork. Then continue ahead and turn left onto a footpath that goes along the side of the river. This will eventually re-join the pathway you left at another fingerpost. Keep following the town centre signs.

3. When the path turns left towards a bridge cross over. This is a favourite spot for locals feeding the swans and ducks. Turn left at the end of the bridge and continue on a footpath to pass by a much older bridge, the Andressey Bridge of 1884. Now follow the path through the garden of remembrance that was created from the old burial ground of St Modwen's Church. Eventually walk along the side of St Modwen's Church to enter Market Place.

4. This is a delightful square and very vibrant when the market is on. Cross the square to reach the war memorial. Look for the name of Lance Corporal Coltman, who was a stretcher bearer during the Great War and was awarded the Victoria Cross, the Distinguished Conduct Medal and Bar and the Military Medal and bar for his most selfless acts of bravery. He was the most decorated other ranks soldier in the British Army. He lived in Burton until he died in 1974.

5. Walk past the memorial towards the Leopard Inn and continue along Lichfield Street. Keep on this as it curves to the left then passes Bond Street. Detour

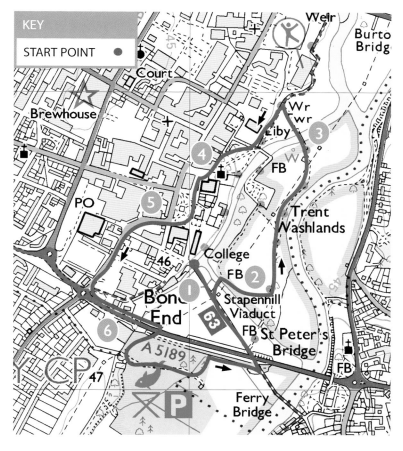

through the car park of St Peter's Retail Park then cross a forecourt to turn left onto the road heading towards St Peter's Bridge.

6. After the filling station veer left onto a track, pass a gate then turn right to go under St Peter's Bridge and continue along a footpath to a T-junction. Turn left again onto a narrow lane and continue along it. When it reaches a park take the left fork of a footpath and follow it left to cross a footbridge. From here a path leads up to the Stapenhill Viaduct. Turn right on this and go along for a little bit to get a view of the Ferry Bridge. Then turn back and keep on the viaduct to return to the start.

LONGNOR

A VERY PRETTY VILLAGE WITH A MARKETPLACE AMIDST THE
BUCOLIC COUNTRYSIDE OF THE PEAK DISTRICT.

Sitting on a limestone ridge between two rivers, the Manifold and the Dove, Longnor was a crossroads for the trade routes that once ran along ridges and linked the earthworks of the ancient people. As such it would have been a favoured meeting spot for early traders to exchange goods and in time it became a significant marketplace. The Lords of Alstonefield Manor had established a market here by the end of the 13th century and in the 16th century John Harpur was granted the right to hold a Tuesday market. This and the various fairs that were held in the town meant that by 1604 it was able to support nine licensed alehouses – and many illegal ones. The major London to Buxton coach routes passing through also benefited the local economy.

At its peak the market would have been a lively, noisy, dirty, smelly event. The 'Table of Tolls' still displayed on the former Market Hall tell us that bulls and cows, sheep, pigs, ducks and other poultry would have been present. Eggs were charged a fee of one penny per basket. Stalls would have sold vegetables, cheese, cloth and household items. This is where the country people from round about would have come for their shopping. The cobbled marketplace was surrounded by pubs, where the cattle drovers, farmers and smallholders would congregate for a drink and to swap gossip. The early market was all on open ground. A building was mooted when the turnpike roads were established but was probably never built and it was not until the early 19th century that one was eventually established. The market house that you see today was built by Sir John Harpur-Crewe in 1873.

By the 20th century Longnor was in decline. Easier access to major centres of population coupled with a decline in agriculture after the Great War meant that people moved away, seeking a better standard of living. Despite this the town still held one of the few remaining hiring fairs in the county. The end of coaching travel, the arrival of motor transport and improved roads meant that much of the trade moved to larger towns. By 1931 the market house had become the parish hall although it is likely that it had ceased to function as a market much earlier.

THE BASICS

Distance: 2¼ miles / 3.6km

Gradient: A couple of slight inclines but mainly flat

Severity: Moderate

Approx. time to walk: 1½ to 1¾ hours

Stiles: Many; most of them are narrow gap stiles

Map: OS Explorer OL 24 (The Peak District, White Peak Area)

Path description: Pavement, grass and dirt footpaths and farm tracks

Start point: In front of the Longnor Craft Centre (GR SK 088649)

Parking: At the start, in the centre of Longnor (free) (SK17 0NT)

Dog friendly: No: too many stiles and grazing cattle

Public toilets: At the start

Nearest food: The excellent Cobbles Coffee Shop at the start (opens early)

1. From the car parking area, cross the road to the Crewe and Harpur Arms, then turn left. Walk along the High Street passing the Post Office and Ye Olde Cheshire Cheese Inn on your left. Pass along a pavement in front of some houses on the right-hand side of the road then turn right down a lane at a way-marker post for the Manifold Trail.

2. Go along the lane to reach Folds End Farm then turn left into the farmyard and proceed towards a set of metal gates at the end. Go through the gate at a public footpath sign and then veer right across a small meadow making for the stile in the bottom corner near a fingerpost.

3. Go over the stile, turn left and follow the path in the direction of Brund via Crofts Farm. The path crosses several meadows, some with cows in them. In all you should encounter six gap stiles, some with small gates. The path is distinct, if narrow and easy to follow. After the first couple of meadows you will see the farm buildings you are heading towards. When you cross the last stile just before the farm, turn sharp right and head down to go through a metal gate with a public footpath sign.

4. Turn left and veer 45 degrees to the right, in front of the farmhouse, to reach a gate beside a large tree. Go through this and follow the path through another meadow, heading for the far corner of a wall in front of you. When you get there continue in the same direction along the side of the wall to reach a marker pole with a faded disc indicating a left turn. Go through the gap stile here, turn sharp right and continue on the path towards another gate. Go through this then follow an indistinct path along the edge of fields, ignoring a track leading to the left, to reach a hedge. The path becomes more distinct here and continues into some bushes to reach a stile. Cross this and continue through more fields to reach a gap stile just before an old stone barn. From there the path leads towards farm buildings ahead.

5. Go across a stile at the farm then veer right to go through a small gate, then turn left to enter the yard and turn left onto the farm access road. Keep on this heading downhill towards another set of farm buildings. Before you reach them you will encounter a way-marker pole on the right. Turn right here and cross the field to reach a gap stile and gate just to the left of the field gate. Go through and cross a meadow, through another stile, over a footbridge and another couple of gap stiles then turn right towards more farm buildings and through another gap stile.

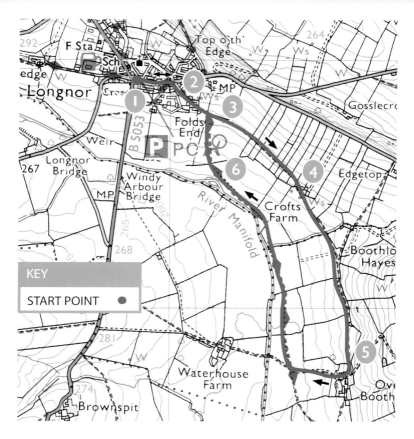

6. From here head steadily back uphill, passing the farm buildings on your left to arrive back at the sign beyond Folds End Farm. Simply re-trace the outer route from here to the car park.

TITTESWORTH RESERVOIR

THIS IS ESSENTIALLY A NATURE WALK BY WATER WITH THE OPPORTUNITY TO SEE A WIDE VARIETY OF BIRDS AND BEASTIES.

The first dam was built here in 1858 to store water from the River Churnet and feed it to the cloth-dying industry in Leek. By the mid-20th century increased demand led to the construction of a much bigger dam and the flooding of farmland to create the reservoir as it is now. Tittesworth Reservoir was completed by 1963. It is the main water supply for the Stoke-on-Trent and Leek area, has a capacity of 6.5 billion gallons of water and can supply 10 million gallons of water every day. The land around it provides a variety of habitats for wildlife. In the visitor centre there's a restaurant and shops as well as an interactive exhibition, where you can find out more about the wildlife and history.

Children will be interested in the brown hares with their distinctive long black legs and black-tipped ears. It's a great opportunity to explain the difference between the hare and the rabbit. You can point out the droppings of otters by the edge of the reservoir, although you probably won't catch sight of one as they tend to be nocturnal. But if you are very quiet, you might spot Ratty from Wind in the Willows. There are lots of water voles here and the holes you spot in the banks are their burrows. Sit or stand for a while where you have a view of one and he might just pop his head out.

Near the end of the reservoir you will pass the Butterfly Beach, created by the water authority to encourage butterflies. It's even got a butterfly hotel, where they can spend the winter, emerging again in the spring. It's a great place to see the beautiful Red Admiral and the equally spectacular Painted Lady amongst others.

The whole area is a paradise for birdwatchers. The birds that you see will obviously depend on the time of year, which is why a field guide is a useful addition to your pack.

There are a couple of hides where you can get much closer to them. Particular birds to look out for are kingfishers, linnets, skylarks, cormorants, pied flycatchers and great crested grebes, and if you are really lucky your visit may coincide with one from a magnificent osprey.

THE BASICS

Distance: 4½ miles / 7.2km

Gradient: A few short steepish sections and lots of undulations

Severity: Moderate

Approx. time to walk: 3 to 3½ hours

Stiles: None

Map: OS Explorer OL24 (The Peak District, White Peak Area)

Path description: Surfaced and grass footpaths, farm road and country lanes. Short section on pavement

Start point: Tittesworth Reservoir Visitor Centre (GR SJ 994602)

Parking: At Tittesworth Reservoir (charge) (ST13 8SW)

Dog friendly: Must be kept on a lead at all times

Public toilets: In the Visitor Centre

Nearest food: Café in Visitor Centre

1. From the visitor centre head across the car park to a sign pointing to the way-marked walks. Pass this to go onto a well-surfaced footpath and continue along it. Ahead of you on the horizon you will see the rocky spine of The Roaches. When the path forks go right to reach a wooded area with a brook running through it. Turn left here, then right across a bridge, across another footbridge and continue on the path to reach a junction with a fingerpost.

2. If you want to stick to the main path you can continue in the direction of the red and yellow walks. Otherwise turn right to take the water's edge path. The path narrows then becomes grassy soon after reaching the water's edge. It also splits again and keeping right will take you to a viewpoint where you can look over the reservoir. Then continue on a narrow grassy path through woodland to re-join the main surfaced footpath and turn right onto it. When you reach a junction with a bridge on your left keep ahead following the fingerpost in the direction of the yellow route. At the next

   fingerpost turn right again to take the water's edge path. This is another grassy track that will eventually re-join the main walk. When it does turn right again and continue following the Yellow Trail.

3. At the halfway point you will encounter a bench informing you that you are halfway round. Keep on the path as it crosses a bridge then heads uphill and then down the other side. Eventually the path will emerge from woodland. Turn left towards the dam at the head of the reservoir. Go through a gate and cross the dam, then climb several sets of steps at the other side to reach a footpath and turn right. Follow this through woodland, then a gate and continue to a T-junction by a fingerpost. Turn right here onto a farm road.

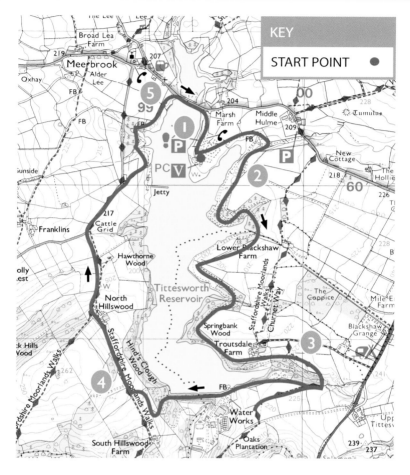

4. Keep on this following signs for Meerbrook to cross a cattle grid and reach a T-junction with a road. Turn right here following the signs for the Visitor Centre. In a short distance turn right at a junction following the signs for the Visitor Centre then turn left onto a footpath by a fingerpost back into the reservoir grounds. Cross several bridges and pass an interesting insect hotel to reach a gate.

5. Go through this onto the main road, cross over and turn right. Continue along the pavement for a short distance to reach the entrance to the reservoir grounds and follow the road back to the Visitor Centre.

LUD'S CHURCH

Follow in the footsteps of Sir Gawain, Knight of the Round Table, in search of the legendary Green Chapel where he had his fateful encounter with the Green Knight.

There's an Arthurian tale, preserved in a 14th-century poem, concerning Sir Gawain, one of the Knights of the Round Table. Gawain accepts a challenge from a mysterious green knight to take off the man's head with one blow of his axe. But the challenge involves Gawain agreeing to accept a similar blow himself a year and a day later. After the beheading the Green Knight picks up his head, reminds Gawain of their bargain, tells him to meet him at the Green Chapel, then departs.

When Gawain sets off to meet the knight the following year, he stops to rest at a castle. The lord gives him directions to the Chapel but invites him to rest for a few days. Over the next three days each morning Gawain's host gets him to agree to swap whatever he gets during the day for the spoils of the hunt. Later the lady of the house tries to seduce him. He fends her off with just one kiss. That night he gives the lord a kiss for a deer. This goes on for another two days, with Gawain receiving two and then three kisses as well as a green and gold silk girdle, which the lady says will protect him from harm. The kisses he passes on to the lord, but not the girdle, which he wears around his waist when he departs for his appointment. When the Green Knight's blow falls, it leaves only a slight wound.

In 1958, after a great deal of research, Professor Ralph Elliott of Keele University identified the deep natural chasm known as Lud's Church as the Chapel of the Green Knight.

As you walk through the forest you will recognise some of the descriptions in the poem: 'wonderfully wild was their way through the woods'. The place was possibly named after Walter de Lud-Auk, one of the dissident followers of the preacher John Wycliffe. Walter held clandestine services here, which were eventually attacked by establishment forces, resulting in the death of his daughter Alice. Apparently she still haunts the place – along with the headless figure of a large Green Knight.

THE BASICS

Distance: 2 miles / 3.2km

Gradient: Some steep and rough sections

Severity: Strenuous

Approx. time to walk: 1½ hours

Stiles: None

Map: OS Explorer OL24 (The Peak District, White Peak Area)

Path description: Rough, eroded footpaths & woodland paths, can be muddy in parts

Start point: Roach End, on minor road just west of A53 (GR SJ 995644)

Parking: Roadside parking near Roach End (nearest postcode ST13 8TA)

Dog friendly: A great dog walk

Public toilets: None on the walk. Nearest at Tittesworth Reservoir Visitor Centre.

Nearest food: None on the walk. Nearest at Tittesworth Water Visitor Centre. There is sometimes an ice cream van parked near Roach End

LUD'S CHURCH

1. From the parking area at Roach End look for a cattle grid. With this behind you and a farm track to your left, head up the road then almost immediately veer left onto grass and follow a well-trodden path to the top where you will find a wooden gate. Go through the gate and head along a rough track that runs across open countryside with a wall to the left. At a junction marked by a fingerpost keep ahead towards Swythamley via Ridge.

2. At the next junction turn right onto a narrow footpath signposted for Lud's Church and Gradbach. Proceed carefully downhill. This path is narrow and eroded in parts, so stout shoes or boots and a walking pole would be good kit to have. Continue to reach the edge of the woods where the path levels out and the going becomes much easier. If you are there at the right time you can also feast on the blueberries that grow here in abundance (unless the foragers have beaten you to it).

3. At a path junction turn left following the sign for Lud's Church and follow this pleasant woodland footpath. There will be a few signs of the chasm you are approaching but way-markers will guide you past all of them to reach a wooden fence where you must turn right. Proceed with caution down a series of rough stone steps. Particular care is required during wet weather. Go slowly and your patience will be well rewarded. Go down more rough steps and explore the length of the chasm before exiting at the other end of it onto a footpath.

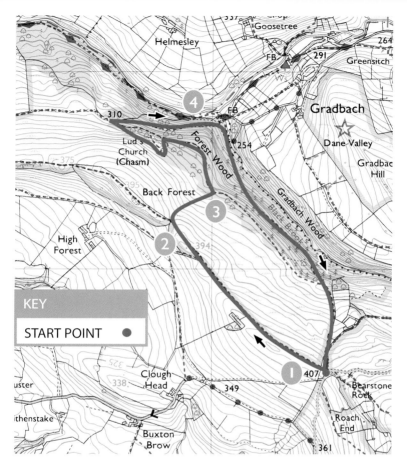

4. Turn right here and take care along several sections of this path where erosion has exposed tree roots. When you reach a junction keep ahead towards The Roaches, and the same at the next junction. Eventually the path will head uphill out of the woods then continue as a stony path to reach the gate near Roach End where you started this walk.

WETTON

THIS IS A WALK THAT TAKES YOU THROUGH THE OPENING
SHOTS OF KEN RUSSELL'S ICONIC 1988 HORROR FILM THE
LAIR OF THE WHITE WORM, WHICH STARRED HUGH
GRANT AND AMANDA DONOHOE.

The Lair of the White Worm was a less well-known book from the pen of Dracula author Bram Stoker and is loosely based on the north-eastern legend of the Lambton Worm, which itself is celebrated by a famous song of the same name.

Peter Capaldi, now better known from Doctor Who, played the part of Angus Flint, an archaeology student, who unearths a strange reptile skull at a dig he is working on. Later he attends the annual celebration of the slaying of the D'Ampton Worm at the home of Lord D'Ampton. Hugh Grant has that role while Amanda Donohoe is cast as the snake-like Lady Sylvia. She worships the snake, which lives in a cavern near Temple Hall, her Gothic mansion. The snake has a taste for young flesh and when Angus's landlady's sister, Eve, disappears following the celebration, D'Ampton suspects that Lady Sylvia has captured her to feed the great worm. He attempts to uncover a tunnel running from the cave to Sylvia's mansion but it is Angus who saves the day, appearing as the stereotypical Scot, clad in a kilt and making a terrible racket playing bagpipes. He has also acquired a hand grenade, which he uses to destroy the worm, saving the day and the young lady. It's a fine piece of hokum. If you watch the film first the actual interior of Thor's Cave is likely to prove something of a disappointment.

Excavations in the 19th and 20th centuries have revealed several human burials and unearthed prehistoric remains including animal bones and various flints that have been dated back to the Neolithic and Bronze ages. Over the years the cave has provided a natural den for a range of wild creatures. Other discoveries suggest that the cave was still in use by humans during the Roman occupation of Britain.

Thor's Cave has a very distinctive arch-like entrance and was created by water eroding the limestone crag in which it is located. It is a famous local landmark and tourist attraction. It even had its own railway station, waiting and refreshment rooms, from 1904 to 1934, when the Manifold Valley Light Railway was in operation. When it ceased the rails were lifted and the trackbed now forms the Manifold Way.

THE BASICS

Distance: 3 miles / 4.8km

Gradient: A steep ascent from the valley to Wetton and a steepish return decent

Severity: Severe

Approx. time to walk: 2 hours

Stiles: Eight

Map: OS Explorer OL24 (The Peak District, White Peak Area)

Path description: Metalled footpath, hill and grass footpaths and farm tracks

Start point: At Weags Bridge on the Manifold Way, just east of Grindon (GR SK 100542)

Parking: On the Manifold Way (nearest postcode is ST13 7TX)

Dog friendly: Must be kept on lead on National Trust land. Dogs may have trouble with the gap stiles and some of the other stiles

Public toilets: At Car Park in Wetton, at Grindon on the other side of the valley or at Wetton Mill

Nearest food: The Royal Oak at Wetton

WETTON WALK

1. From the car park head along the tarmac Manifold Way in the opposite direction from Weag's Bridge. You will soon reach a gate and a sign prohibiting motorised transport. This is the line of the old railway and you should continue walking along it until you reach Ladyside, which is marked on the left by a National Trust sign.

2. Turn right onto a footpath and walk past the interpretation board for Thor's Cave. Continue over a bridge then along a footpath, which rises steadily uphill through woodland. When you reach a junction at a fingerpost turn right and follow the path uphill to explore Thor's Cave, then return to this point and continue in the direction of Wetton.

3. Exit the woods through a gate and keep ahead uphill on a well-defined footpath, heading for a gap in the trees, then through a gate to reach the village, where you cross through a gap stile and turn right onto the road. Walk through Wetton then turn right at a sign pointing to Grindon. Almost immediately turn right to cross a stile into the garden of a farmhouse. Keep to the path that runs by the right-hand side of the buildings and exit the garden over another stile. Follow a narrow path that passes to the right of some farm buildings, crosses a stile by a metal gate then heads along a farm track (possibly through another gate) to reach a gap stile to the left of a gate and open fields beyond.

4. Follow the path through this stile and three others to reach a lane then turn right and head downhill. At a fingerpost on the right go through a gate and onto another footpath through fields, this time heading downhill to cross a stile onto the lane again. Cross a cattle grid then turn left through a gap stile at a fingerpost and head downhill through yet another field. Ahead of you is Beeston Tor. This is now National Trust Property so if you have a dog it must be kept on a lead. Eventually at the bottom of this field cross through a gap stile and onto a footpath through woodland.

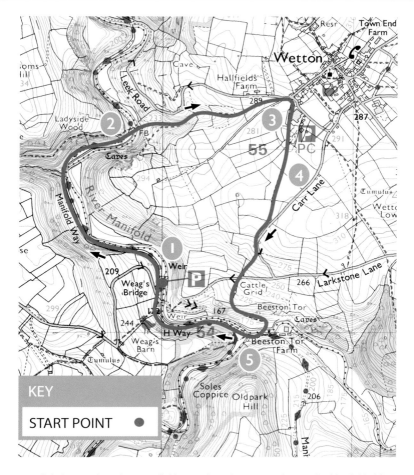

Exit the woods and cross a field to go through a gate and cross the Manifold. Often this is a dry riverbed but if it is running turn left to reach the stepping stones.

5. Turn right on the other side of the Manifold and continue to reach a caravan site. Go through this, keeping to the right, then exit onto the lane and follow that past Weag's Bridge back to the start.

BARLASTON

Take a picturesque village, a canalside walk with ubiquitous grey herons, fishing ponds, woodland, meadows and the Wedgwood Visitor Centre and you have the makings of the perfect walk.

The world-famous pottery company founded by Josiah Wedgwood in 1759 at Burslem in Stoke-on-Trent has moved home twice. In 1766, Josiah purchased the estate of Etruria, took up residence in the mansion and by 1769 his company was operating from the site as well. The final move was in the late 1930s when the company purchased the Barlaston Estate and constructed a purpose-built modern factory in the grounds.

In 1945 they opened the Wedgwood Memorial College in Barlaston Hall. Damage from mining subsidence forced them to move it to other properties in the village, which you will pass on the walk. Until it closed in 2012 it offered a variety of courses, including Esperanto. The Centre for Esperanto and the headquarters of the Esperanto Association of Britain are still based there.

The Hall is a Palladian country house built in red brick, around the mid-18th century, for Thomas Mills, a lawyer in nearby Leek. The architect Sir Robert Taylor had a penchant for octagonal and diamond glazing and the Hall is now one of the few buildings that retain this feature. The estate passed by marriage to the Adderley family in 1816 and in 1937 was sold to Wedgwood, but the company's connection with the Hall goes back further. It featured in the design of a dish that was part of a 925-piece dinner service in the famous creamware that Josiah created for Catherine the Great of Russia.

The Wedgwood Company continued to maintain the Hall after the college had to move out, but as vandalism and mining subsidence took its toll it was eventually sold for just one pound to Save Britain's Heritage. Following the threat of litigation the National Coal Board agreed to pay compensation and fund the construction of a concrete raft under the house.

All of the external restoration was completed by the time it was sold in 1992. The new owners have recreated the original interior but it is a private family house and not open to visitors.

Just beyond it is the old parish church, dedicated to St John the Baptist. Although it is Victorian the west tower is medieval. Unfortunately it suffered from the same mining subsidence as its neighbour and closed permanently in 1981.

THE BASICS

Distance: 3 miles / 4.8km

Gradient: Slight, almost flat

Severity: Easy

Approx. time to walk: 3 hours

Stiles: Five

Map: OS Explorer 258 (Stoke-on-Trent and Newcastle-under-Lyme)

Path description: Pavements, canal towpath and field footpaths

Start point: The Duke of York on Longton Road in Barlaston (GR SJ 894384)

Parking: On-street parking in Longton Road near the Duke of York (ST12 9AA)

Dog friendly: Stiles make this rather unfriendly for dogs

Public toilets: None on the walk

Nearest food: The Duke of York

BARLASTON WALK

1. Turn left from outside the Duke of York and head down Longton Road passing the village hall on the right. Turn right at the junction into Station Road and walk along the pavement. When you reach the railway, take care crossing over. Then continue along the street to cross the canal bridge and turn right just before the Plume of Feathers pub, to get onto the canal towpath. Walk along it to Bridge 104.

2. Leave the canal here and turn right to cross the canal bridge then continue along Wedgwood Drive. Cross the railway line again at Wedgwood Station and continue on the road to reach a bridge just before Queen Mary's Drive.

3. Turn right here and go through a gate onto a private footpath on the Wedgwood Estate. A sign informs you that the public are welcome to use the path but dogs must be kept on a lead. Walk along the side of a very pretty lake then, as you round the end, veer left onto a narrow footpath that heads into the woods.  Follow this path through the woods to cross a stile, then turn left along the edge of another lake. Look out for a way-marker disc on a fence by the next lot of woods and cross a stile onto another footpath that just skirts the woods then exits via another stile into a meadow.

4. Veer right in the direction indicated by the marker and head towards a large tree on the horizon. Cross a fence by another stile and keep ahead over another stile. Keep going in the same direction and the village should now be visible.

5. Go through a kissing gate then turn right and head back down Longton Road to the start.

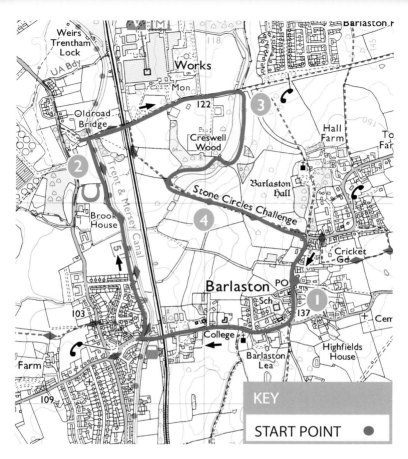

KEY

START POINT ●

MILWICH

Milwich is a pretty little village with thatched cottages, a decent pub and an interesting churchyard. Most of this walk is through pleasant meadows and along quiet country lanes.

There's been a settlement here as far back as 1086, when it is mentioned in the Domesday Book as Mulewiche. A couple of centuries later it was owned by two landowners, Robert de Milwich and Geoffrey de Nugent. The main manor house was Milwich Hall. It's a timber-framed building from the late 16th or early 17th century. It was built on the site of the original Saxon hall and was surrounded by a moat. The timber framing was concealed under plaster until it was removed in the 1970s.

One of the first buildings you will encounter on this walk is the village hall. It was originally the National School, built in 1833, and despite being a very small building had a separate school for boys and the other for girls and infants, their doors separated by just a few feet. A new school opened in nearby Coton in 1929 and the old school closed.

The main building of interest in the village is the parish church of All Saints. Its substantial Victorian vicarage, built in 1853, is now in private hands. It replaced an earlier thatched building, which was in a poor state of repair. The main claim to fame of the local church is its having the oldest bell in Staffordshire and the seventh oldest in England, cast in 1409 by John of Colsale. There are only two surviving medieval bells that bear both the name of the founder and the date of creation. This is one of them. The church was built in 1792 on the site previously occupied by the original medieval church. The tower, although substantially rebuilt in the late 15th century, is the only part of the medieval church to have survived. The gallery was added in 1837 and the pitch pine panelling is from 1888.

Inside the church, the font is particularly interesting. It's from the 13th century and bears the scars of the vandalism that was carried out at the time of the Reformation, when a lot of decoration was obliterated.

The oldest memorial can be spotted just inside the church. Look up and see the gravestone of the 12th-century Lord of the Manor, Nicholas of Milwich, who was also the priest here.

THE BASICS

Distance: 3 miles / 4.8km

Gradient: Slight; mostly flat

Severity: Moderate

Approx. time to walk: 2 hours

Stiles: Six

Map: OS Explorer 258 (Stoke-on-Trent and Newcastle-under-Lyme)

Path description: Country lanes, grass tracks and footpaths through meadows

Start point: Milwich Village Hall (GR SJ 971323)

Parking: At the village hall in Milwich (ST18 0EG)

Dog friendly: Probably too many stiles

Public toilets: There are toilets in the church and at The Green Man

Nearest food: The Green Man, Milwich

MILWICH WALK

1. Leave the car park and turn left to go along the B5027, passing the old school on your left and The Green Man on the junction to your right. Continue through the village passing a left turn into The Allways on your left and then, just after the road curves right, turn left into Postman's Lane.

2. Look out on the right-hand side for a public footpath post just as the lane curves slightly to the left. Turn right here to go through a gate and onto a broad, grassy track. After a short distance turn right over a way-marked stile and head across a meadow, keeping to the left of an old overgrown hedge. This will lead to another stile. Cross it and keep ahead. As this field opens out veer right to reach a footbridge. Go over it and turn left. Follow the edge of the field to cross another stile. The path then becomes more distinct as it crosses another meadow to exit over a stile onto the road.

3. Turn right and walk along this road passing the turn off for the village of Coton and the ruins of the Wheatsheaf Inn. The road bends right here and heads uphill. Cross the road, just past some farm buildings on your left, and cross a stile into a meadow. Keep on a straight line towards the left side of a hedge. Walk along it and downhill to go through a gate into the next meadow, cross it to reach a footbridge leading into the next field, turn right to cross a stile then continue right along the edge of this field to reach a kissing gate into the churchyard.

4. Exit the churchyard onto a lane, turn right and follow it to a junction with another lane. Turn right again and head downhill into the village to arrive at the junction by The Green Man. From here return to the car park.

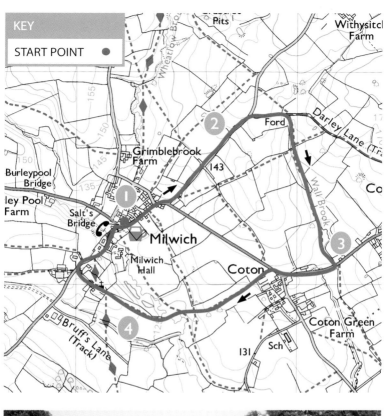

KEY

START POINT ●

GREAT HAYWOOD

GREAT HAYWOOD IS A VILLAGE ON THE RIVER TRENT, NOT FAR FROM RUGELEY, WITH A FAMOUS STATELY HOME AND A CANAL NETWORK.

The great canal engineer, James Brindley, devised a scheme he called the 'Grand Cross' to link the rivers Trent, Mersey, Severn and Thames. Part of this scheme was the 'Grand Trunk', linking the Mersey to the Trent, providing the northern and eastern arms of his cross. The Staffordshire and Worcester was the western arm. The junction created at Great Haywood, together with Fradley Junction, formed the central hub, just like a modern motorway interchange.

The Staffordshire and Worcester Canal widens at Tixall Wide to appear like a lake. This was because the owner of Tixall Hall refused to have a 'muddy ditch' on his property but agreed to let the canal through provided they created an acceptable lake. Look across the lake to see the ornate 16th-century gatehouse that is all that remains of Tixall Hall, which was demolished in 1927. The gatehouse, which is three stories high, dates from around 1580 and looks like a mansion in its own right.

Shugborough Hall is a great stately home and seat of the Anson family, Earls of Lichfield. In 1950 the then 5th Earl, the photographer, Patrick Lichfield, gave the estate to the National Trust in lieu of death duties but for his lifetime retained the use of several rooms in the house. Now run by Staffordshire County Council it is open to the public.

In 2011 Lichfield's private apartments were opened as an attraction. If you have time to see just a small part of the estate then this is it. The rooms are furnished as they would have been when he used them. His London photographic studio has been re-created in one of them and as you would expect there are lots of his photographs on display.

The former servants' quarters are now Staffordshire County Museum. It's a living history museum and the highlights include the Victorian kitchen, a working laundry, an incredible collection of carriages and England's only log-fired brewery, which actually does produce beer.

Towards the end of the walk you cross the Trent via the 16th-century Essex Bridge. It's only a few feet wide, with fourteen arches, and is one of the longest surviving packhorse bridges in England. It was built around 1550 by the Earl of Essex, hence the name.

THE BASICS

Distance: 4 miles / 6.4 km

Gradient: Mostly flat with the exception of a long, slow, gentle, climb at point (5)

Severity: Easy

Approx time to walk: 2 to 2½ hours

Stiles: None

Maps: OS Explorer 244 (Cannock Chase and Chasewater)

Path description: Canal towpath, pavement, roadside and dirt footpaths

Start point: Outside the Clifford Arms, Great Haywood (GR SJ 997226)

Parking: Roadside parking in Great Haywood or at the Clifford Arms (ST18 0SR)

Dog friendly: An excellent dog walk

Public toilets: None on the route. Use the pub and cafes

Nearest food: Clifford Arms, Lock House Restaurant and Tea Barn and Ladywalk Tea Rooms (all on the walk)

GREAT HAYWOOD WALK

1. Facing the Clifford Arms turn left, and head along a short street and under a railway bridge. Cross the bridge over the canal and turn left onto the towpath of the Trent and Mersey Canal, then left again to go under Bridge 73 onto the Queen's Golden Jubilee Walk.

2. Walk along the towpath going under the Swivel Bridge and keep going to reach Great Haywood Junction, where the Staffordshire and Worcester Canal joins the Trent and Mersey. Turn left here, under the very distinctive Haywood Bridge No. 109, and head in the direction of Wolverhampton.

© NTPL / Nick Meers

3. In a short distance you will walk along the path by an aqueduct carrying the canal over the River Trent. Keep walking along the towpath. Eventually you will come to a much wider part of the canal called the Tixall Wide. Pass this and continue to reach Oldhill Bridge and beyond them Tixall Lock with its distinctive white lockkeeper's cottage. Shortly afterwards reach Tixall Bridge, No. 106. Go under it then turn left and go up some steps onto the road.

4. Walk carefully along this quiet road, crossing a bridge over the River Sow and then another over the railway to reach a junction with the A513. At the junction is the entrance to Shugborough, complete with 18th-century lodges. Ignore this and turn left along the A513. Keep going until you reach a footpath sign on the left beside a gravel layby and turn onto the path.

5. Head uphill through woodland. This is the only real incline on the walk but just take your time and it will present little difficulty. When the grass track reaches a junction keep left. Then at another junction keep right. Eventually head downhill to reach a barrier at another junction. Go round this and keep left past the car park to reach the A513 again. Turn left and walk along the pavement. When a house appears on your right look for a footpath sign on your left then turn left to go through a gate and along a short track to go through another gate onto the main access road into Shugborough.

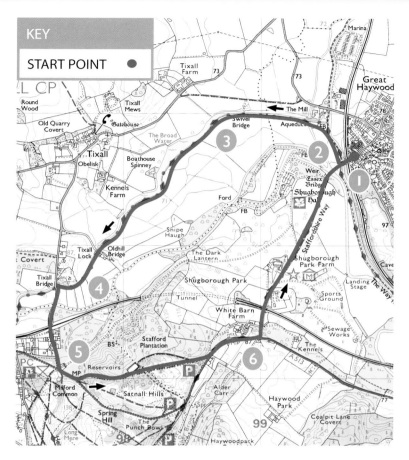

KEY

START POINT ●

6. This is the Staffordshire Way, which runs through the estate, passing the entrance on the right. When the road forks, keep left then, where it bends, keep ahead on a much narrower footpath to pass Shugborough House, then onwards to cross Essex Bridge, the canal bridge and back to the start.

ETRURIA

This is the very heart of 'The Potteries', where Josiah Wedgwood industrialised pottery manufacture.

Pottery is a delicate product and packhorse transport in the 18th century was rough and ready, causing a high percentage of damage. Transporting goods by boat would reduce the damage and increase profits, so Wedgwood was particularly keen to have a canal system that was easily accessible from his factory. He wanted a canal that would link the rivers Trent and Mersey and open up his overseas markets. James Brindley, the engineer, designed the scheme. Wedgwood lobbied Parliament to achieve it and in 1766 it was authorised by an Act of Parliament. This was Brindley's first canal, although he had previously consulted on the Bridgewater Canal and the Trent and Mersey.

At the same time Wedgwood was having a new house built. Etruria Hall was built between 1768 and 1771 and was Josiah's home until his death in 1795. His son Thomas continued to live there, conducting his pioneering photographic experiments. The Hall was sold in the 1840s and is now part of the Moat House Hotel. The Wedgwood Company moved from here to nearby Barlaston in the late 1930s and the industry is now a shadow of its former self. On the walk you can see the industrial remains, including a particularly fine pair of distinctive bottle kilns by the canalside surrounded by houses.

The Etruria Industrial Museum is housed in what used to be Jesse Shirley's Bone and Flint Mill at Etruria Junction. Shirley went into business in 1820; by 1837 he was supplying Wedgwood and the company is still in business today. It's the world's oldest supplier of calcined bone ash for the fine china industry. It was built in 1857 and ground the cattle bones and the flint that were essential ingredients for fine bone china. Now fully restored, it includes a calcinating kiln, grinding pans and a steam engine that was in operation until 1972, when the company moved to new premises. Above the mill is the old forge, which has been rebuilt on the site it has occupied for 150 years.

It operated into the 1960s and is still used by a blacksmith, who gives demonstrations on open weekends. A canal warehouse and check office completes the museum complex. Just across the Caldon Canal from the museum entrance is a bronze statue of James Brindley, builder of the canal.

THE BASICS

Distance: 3½ miles / 5.6km

Gradient: Mainly flat, but slight gradients beside locks

Severity: Easy

Approx. time to walk: 2 hours

Stiles: None

Map: OS Explorer 258 (Stoke-on-Trent and Newcastle-under-Lyme)

Path description: Canal towpath, pavement and paved areas

Start point: Car park beside the marina and Toby Carvery, Festival Park, just off the A53 (GR SJ 869475)

Parking: Pay and display car park beside the Toby Carvery (ST1 5PA)

Dog friendly: Yes, provided you keep it on a lead where instructed

Toilets: Hanley Park on the walk

Nearest food: Toby Carvery on the car park. Costa Coffee a couple of hundred metres away by the cinema and other restaurants on Festival Park

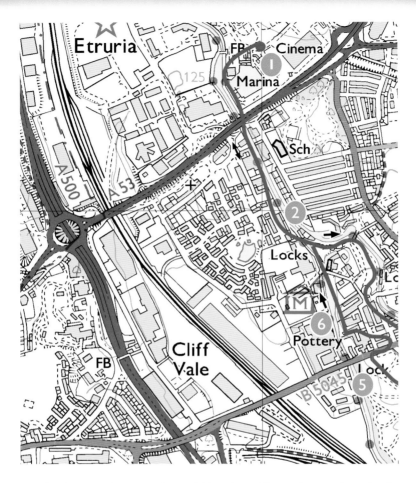

1. Exit the car park, cross to the canalside and turn left onto the towpath passing the Toby Carvery. Then cross a drawbridge by the marina. At the road bridge go across it, down the other side then turn right to continue along the towpath. When you reach the Etruria Industrial Museum this is the junction where the Trent and Mersey meets the Caldon Canal. Cross the bridge at the locks here then veer left between the museum buildings to get onto the towpath of the Caldon Canal.

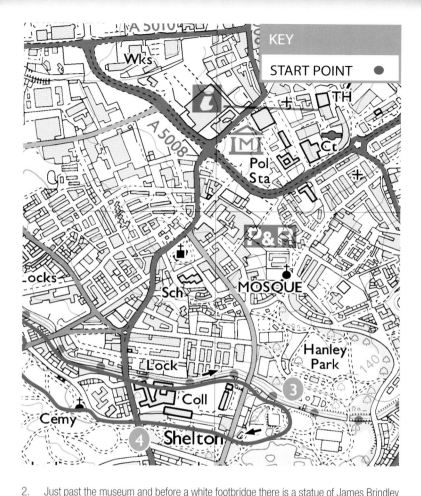

KEY

START POINT ●

2. Just past the museum and before a white footbridge there is a statue of James Brindley on the opposite side of the canal. To the right of the footbridge a sign marks the site of North Staffordshire's first hospital, built in 1804. Continue from here along the canal, passing locks and going under several bridges to reach Hanley Park, just before the blue bridge number 5A.

3. Turn right into the park and head down through it to reach an ornate lake. There are

lots of geese and ducks round this part. Turn right and take the path towards a large exit gate. Go through it, carefully cross the road then go through another gate and onto paths through gardens running alongside Stoke College. Exit via a gate, cross the road then turn left into Cemetery Road and walk along it to the main entrance and ornate gates of the cemetery.

4. Go through the arch and keep roughly ahead to reach the bank of the canal. Turn right and walk along here, looking out for two old bottle kilns on the other side of the canal. Then walk to the end of the cemetery, up a set of steps and turn right onto the road.

5. Head uphill, cross the road and turn into Castlefield Street, then left into Lower Bedford Street, then left along a lane with a museum sign to arrive at the canalside in front of a flint and bone works.

6. Turn right onto this towpath, climb up steps by the lock then keep on to the locks at the museum. From here re-trace your steps to the start.

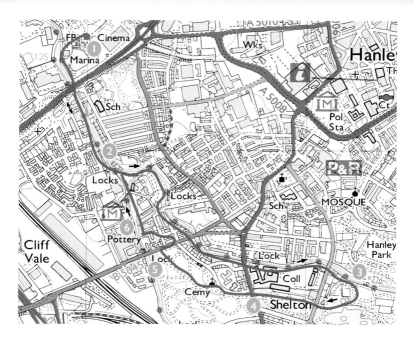

CHEDDLETON

A restored railway and an industrial heritage walk along the banks of the Caldon Canal with an excellent waterside Inn.

The Caldon Canal is a branch of the Trent and Mersey Canal. A mere eighteen miles (29km) long, it runs from Etruria Junction to Froghall. Just past Cheddleton Locks and Bridge 43 is The Old Dock House where Cheddleton's Methodist congregation met from 1790. Just after Bridge 42 is The Old Flint Mill, which is now a museum. We were lucky that it was open and one of the volunteers was present to show us round as it is only normally open at weekends and bank holidays.

Milling has taken place on this spot since 1150 when water from the River Churnet was first used to grind corn. By 1580 a second wheel had been added to run a fulling mill. During the Industrial Revolution the corn mill was adapted to grind flint and a second mill was constructed behind it for the same purpose. The museum now includes both buildings, two flint kilns, a drying kiln and the miller's cottage, complete with range and table set for a meal. Inside the smaller mill building the machinery is still in place and interpretation boards explain the process of preparing the flint for use and how the pottery industry came to be based in Staffordshire.

Towards the end of the walk is the other major attraction in the area: The Churnet Valley Railway. Cheddleton Station is a fine Victorian building, which first opened in 1849 on the Churnet Valley Line. Traffic declined from the mid-20th century and in 1963 it was one of the casualties of Dr Beeching's infamous cuts. In 1974 the local council decided to demolish the station buildings. Norman Hancock, a local businessman, parked his car on the level crossing to prevent the bulldozers getting access. Some hurried lobbying, involving local groups, the Victorian Society and Sir John Betjeman, resulted in the building getting Grade II listed status a month later and ensuring it could be leased to a railway preservation society as a museum. When the railway line closed to traffic in 1988, the society purchased it and ran their first service in 1996. The Churnet Valley Railway now runs along just over ten miles of track. Norman Hancock died on 30 November 1995 and a plaque fixed to the station house wall commemorates his heroic action.

THE BASICS

Distance: 2 miles / 3.2km
Gradient: Mainly flat level going
Severity: Easy
Approx time to walk: 1½ hours
Stiles: None
Maps: OS Explorer 258 (Stoke-on-Trent and Newcastle-under-Lyme)
Path description: Canal towpath, footpath and pavement
Start Point: The Boat Inn in Basford Bridge Lane, Cheddleton (GR SJ 981520)
Parking: Car park at the Boat Inn (ST13 7EQ)
Dog friendly: On leads for preference
Public toilets: Deep Hayes Country Park
Nearest food: Boat Inn

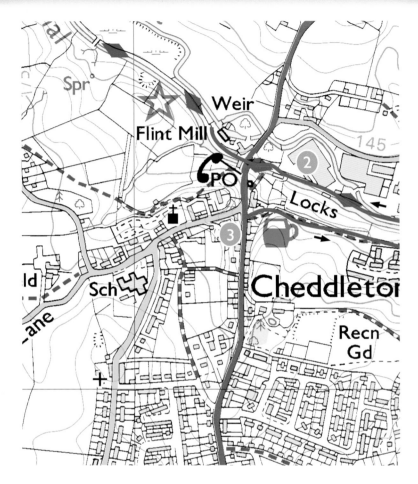

1. From the car park at the Boat Inn, cross the road and walk to the side of the bridge to reach the canal towpath. Walk to the right along this, heading away from the pub. Go past a lock, and look out on the other side of the canal for The Old Dock House. A plaque on the gable will tell you that this was 'the first real home of Methodism in Cheddleton' with Sunday services being held in the building from the 1790s. Go under a bridge (No. 42) and go along the towpath to reach the Flint

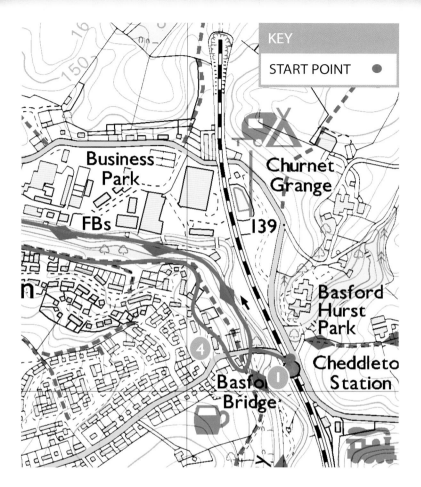

Mill. If you are lucky and it's open then spend some time looking around inside. The cottage gives a fascinating insight into how life was lived long ago. It's free but donations are always appreciated.

2. When you have seen all you want, return to the bridge but instead of going under, keep left and head up to the road where you should turn right onto a pavement. Head uphill, passing the Red Lion, to reach a junction with a road on the right. Turn left here, cross the road and go onto a public footpath to Basford Bridge.

3. Keep on this footpath passing through two kissing gates. When you reach a junction of paths go right and head uphill on another path. When it emerges onto a road amongst some houses turn left and go along the pavement.

4.   A short distance along on the right a narrow footpath heads off to the left across a grassy area. Take it. This will emerge at a gravel area near some lock-ups. Keep ahead to pass in front of a row of cottages in Basford Bridge Terrace, to reach the main road just opposite the Boat Inn. Turn left here, head downhill, across the bridge and along the road to arrive at Cheddleton Station.

5.   A heritage railway runs steam trips here at weekends. If you are there during the week just have a look around and then re-trace your steps to the Boat Inn and the start of the walk.

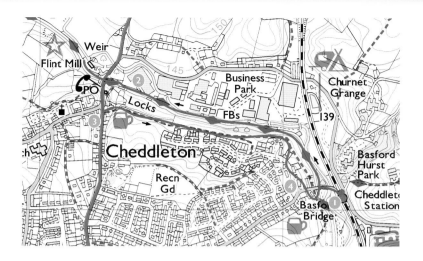

TRYSULL

LIKE MANY OF THE OTHER WALKS IN STAFFORDSHIRE THIS
ONE COMBINES INDUSTRIAL HERITAGE WITH PEACEFUL
COUNTRYSIDE.

The Victorians had a penchant for constructing buildings to house municipal utilities and disguising them as fairy-tale castles. Bratch Pumping Station is one such. Built in 1895 it has over-the-top, ornate brickwork complete with turrets on all four corners. It looks more like a small castle or Gothic church than the industrial building it is. It once had a splendid Italianate chimneystack but that has been dismantled. It was constructed following a dispute between two authorities. Bilston Council thought it was being charged too much for water by Wolverhampton and created the station to pump pure drinking water from boreholes deep in the ground. It served the community well for over 65 years until a new waterworks was built but the site is still used for water extraction. You will pass it on the left-hand side of Bratch Lane on your way to the canal.

It still contains its two steam pumps, one restored. A voluntary heritage group, The Friends of Bratch, held public steamings on a few weekends each year. Unfortunately they are considering disbanding because of lack of access to the site, which is still owned by the Severn and Trent. Bratch is one of only fifty steam pumping stations remaining in England and it's in a poor state of repair, prompting the local MP to pressurise the water company and English Heritage to rectify the situation.

The Bratch locks system, designed by James Brindley, is probably the most impressive feature on the walk. Opened in 1772 as a three-lock staircase, it was later altered to form three separate locks. The first building is the Toll House with the St George's Cross flying from its flagpole. It's a fine example of Georgian architecture, as is the keeper's cottage, which is constructed from the same local red brick.

Near the end of the walk along the old railway track bed, you will come to Wombourne railway station. It was part of a branch line of the Great Western Railway from just before the Great War until it stopped carrying passengers in 1932. It continued to carry goods and was used to transport troops and materials during World War II. The line finally succumbed to the Beeching Axe in 1965 and is now the South Staffordshire Railway Walk.

THE BASICS

Distance: 2¼ miles / 3.6km
Gradient: Mostly flat
Severity: Easy
Approx. time to walk: 1¼ hours
Stiles: None
Map: OS Explorer 219 (Wolverhampton and Dudley)
Path description: Canal towpath, country lane, old railway trackbed
Start point: The Railway Café in Wombourne (GR SO 870938)
Parking: At the start, near the Railway Café (WV5 8DW)
Dog friendly: Yes
Public toilets: No public toilets on route. Toilets at Railway Café
Nearest food: The Railway Cafe

TRYSULL WALK

1. From the car park head along the access road to reach the main road and turn right onto Bratch Lane. Walk along this, under a railway bridge, past a row of houses, across another bridge then cross a third bridge, over the canal, and turn right through a gate to reach Bratch Locks.

2. Walk up the side of the locks. There's a small shop at the top where you can buy souvenirs. Then head along the canal towpath away from the locks. Enjoy the walk along the canal through open countryside until you reach Awbridge Bridge, No. 49. Leave the canal here by walking past Awbridge Lock then turning back onto the ramp up to the bridge and the road.

3. Turn left and walk along a quiet country lane. At the junction of Union Lane with Flash Lane turn right and go along Flash Lane. As you approach a railway bridge the lane runs downhill and at times of rain this part of the road is often flooded. But don't worry. Turn right, just before it, onto a narrow footpath that heads up onto the banking and walk along beside a fence to reach the old railway.

4. Turn right again onto a well-surfaced footpath running along the railway trackbed. This is long and straight and lined with trees. Occasionally you will get a glimpse of the surrounding meadows and you will come across strategically placed picnic tables. When you reach the old railway platform you are nearing the end of the walk. The station buildings have been converted into the Railway Café. Just past here turn left to reach the car park.

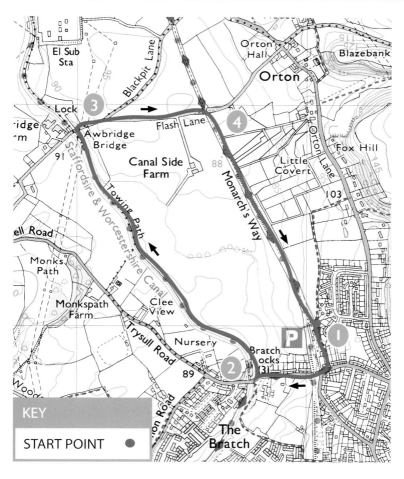

KEY

START POINT ●

CANNOCK CHASE

A WALK THROUGH LOVELY WOODLAND TO THE REMAINS OF AN
IRON AGE FORT.

There are more impressive Iron Age forts in Britain, where the defensive ramparts can be seen more clearly and the vantage point on a hill is more obvious. But the walk through delightful woodland to get here and the views as you walk carefully round the paths are well worth the effort.

In the later Iron Age these protective hill forts were common and within a stockade there would usually have been a number of small wattle and daub dwellings, huddled closely together. Typically each would have been one room, with a fire and a hole in the roof to allow smoke to escape. The fire would have been the centre of the house, providing heat, light and cooking. Meat could also be smoked by hanging it in the rafters of the house. Iron Age people grew barley and rye, made beer and used the yeast for bread, baking it in simple clay, domed ovens.

Castle Ring was probably built over 2,000 years ago, when the ramparts would have been considerably higher, although there are still parts that are over 13 feet (4 m) high. There would have been a wooden stockade on top and the people who lived here would have farmed, growing crops and keeping animals, and of course smelted iron.

It sits on a small hill at the highest point of Cannock Chase. There are commanding views over the Trent Valley and Beaudesert Old Park, which you pass through on the walk. This was a deer park for Beaudesert Hall, whose name, from the French, suggests a beautiful and wild place. When you are in the middle of it, you can well understand that. There are countless paths running in every direction through trees and undergrowth. You can't really get lost but it does feel like an overgrown wilderness.

Unfortunately, the easy accessibility of Castle Ring made this an attractive destination for the Victorians and they drove several paths across and around the monument and even cut into the ramparts.

However, you can still clearly see the ramparts and walk all the way around the top of them, taking care not to go onto the embankments, as they will be eroded by the passage of feet. The aerial views on the interpretation boards give a good idea of what this settlement would have been like.

THE BASICS

Distance: 3 miles / 4.8km

Gradient: Several fairly easy climbs and descents

Severity: Moderate

Approx. time to walk: 1½ hours

Stiles: None

Map: OS Explorer 244 (Cannock Chase and Chasewater)

Path description: Stony forest paths

Start point: Beaudesert Old Park car park (GR SK 035140)

Parking: Beaudesert Old Park car park (WS15 1QW)

Dog friendly: Yes

Public toilets: None

Nearest food: Pub at Castle Ring

CANNOCK CHASE WALK

1. Take a stony path out of the car park around a vehicle gate, heading east parallel to the road. Ignore the narrow track to the left of the forest road. Continue to a crossroads of paths and turn right.

2. Continue along this forest road, passing a pond on the right and crossing a bridge. When you come to a fork, keep right. Shortly after that there is a way-marker for the Heart of England Way and Two Saints' Way. The way-markers are fairly sparse on this route. Continue ahead as another path joins from the left. Shortly the path dips and then climbs steadily.

3. Look out for a narrow path forking to the left. You can take this rough path or continue to a crossroads with a better path to the left. Either way you come to a crossroads of paths. If you took the rough fork you continue ahead; if you took the second path you will be turning left. Go on along this pretty path through the woods until you reach the car park at Castle Ring. Take some time to walk round the remains of this large Iron Age fort and then leave the car park by a way-marked footpath to the left of the entrance to the fort. Follow this path until it reaches a junction then turn left.

4. Keep ahead at a crossroads of paths then keep on it to reach a track at a junction. Keep ahead, taking the track that skirts the right-hand side of a wood. At the next junction keep ahead again. To your left will be a gate and beyond it a small lake. Keep on this track to eventually reach a gate and beyond it a car park.

5. Turn right just before the gate onto a narrow footpath that runs through woodland, parallel to the road. This will lead you back to the car park at the start of the walk.

LICHFIELD IS FAMOUS FOR ITS CATHEDRAL, THE ONLY MEDIEVAL ONE IN EUROPE WITH THREE SPIRES, AND AS THE HOME OF DR SAMUEL JOHNSON.

On a wall in Lichfield Cathedral is a marble memorial to a remarkable woman, Lady Mary Wortley Montagu. She introduced to this country the practice of inoculating against smallpox and used it successfully on her own children. She was an unconventional and highly intelligent English aristocrat, who learned the Turkish language, when she lived there with her husband, the ambassador. She discovered from the local women that they used liquid from a smallpox blister to cure the disease. Having lost her brother to smallpox and having become disfigured by it herself, she decided to inoculate her son. On her return to England she found considerable resistance to the practice. But in 1721 during another epidemic she had her daughter treated and persuaded Princess Caroline to test the treatment on condemned men. They survived and the king's grandchildren were then treated. In the 1790s Edward Jenner, who had been a teenager when Lady Mary died, introduced a safer method of inoculation using cowpox. Lady Mary had no connection with Lichfield, the memorial having been erected, in gratitude, by someone who had benefited from the practice.

Beacon Park, a stone's throw from the cathedral, has another memorial to someone with no connection to Lichfield. It is the bronze statue of Commander Edward John Smith, the master of the ill-fated Titanic, who went down with his ship on 15 April 1912. At the time an appeal was raised to erect a statue in his home town of Stoke, but all they managed was a plaque in Hanley Town Hall in 1913. However some wealthy Americans raised funds for a proper memorial and Lady Kathleen Scott, widow of Scott of the Antarctic, was commissioned to produce it. The statue was sculpted and cast in bronze and was to be mounted on a granite plinth, when Stoke decided they already had a memorial to Smith and refused to accept it. Lichfield decided to take it, although there was some protest from locals. Now ,after several films and a centenary, there is once again great interest in the Titanic and the people of Stoke would like to have the captain after all. Someone started a campaign to have it moved, but Lichfield is not for budging. Captain Smith is a tourist attraction and they are keeping him.

THE BASICS

Distance: 2½ miles / 4km

Gradient: Flat

Severity: Easy

Approx. time to walk: 1½ to 2 hours

Stiles: None

Map: OS Explorer 232 (Nuneaton and Tamworth)

Path description: Pavements, lanes and park footpaths

Start point: Backcester Lane Car park, Lichfield (GR SK 120095)

Start point: Backcester Lane car park, Lichfield (WS13 6HJ)

Dog friendly: Yes

Public toilets: Beacon Park (near the entrance) and throughout the city centre

Nearest food: Many outlets in the city centre near the start of the walk

LICHFIELD WALK

© Rob Farrow

1. From the car park enter the Three Spires Shopping Centre. Turn right and keep going to reach a junction opposite Mr Simms' Olde Sweetie Shoppe. Please note that the authors accept no responsibility for your actions should you enter this shop. Turn right then immediately left into Conduit Street.

2. Go along this street to reach Market Street and turn left into it. In the Market Place you will see statues to James Boswell, the biographer of Dr Johnson, and at the other side of the square the good doctor himself, on a plinth opposite the house in which he was born.

3. Return to the statue of Boswell and turn left into Dam Street. This is an extension of Conduit Street. Turn right to explore some of the ancient houses in Quonians Lane then return to Dam Street and along it to pass Minster Pool. Take the next right onto Reeve Lane.

4. This will take you on a stroll round Stowe Pool, which was originally part of the Bishop's Manorial Rights. They were transferred to the city by Elizabeth I in 1598 and in 1855 became the city water supply after being leased in perpetuity to the South Staffordshire Water Company. They were returned to the city in 1969 and are now part of a popular walk. When you have been round the pool return to Reeve Lane and turn left back along Dam Street.

5. Then turn right onto Minster Pool Walk past the site of Lichfield Speakers Corner. Continue along the length of the pool to reach a road junction. Cross over here and enter Beacon Park. The toilets are to the left of the gate.

6. Enjoy a leisurely stroll around the park looking at the gardens and the statues. The first one you'll find is of King Edward VII, which was presented to the city in 1908 by the then Sheriff of Lichfield. To the right of this is Erasmus Darwin, physician, scientist, poet and inventor, who lived here in the second half of the 18th century. He was the grandfather of Charles Darwin.

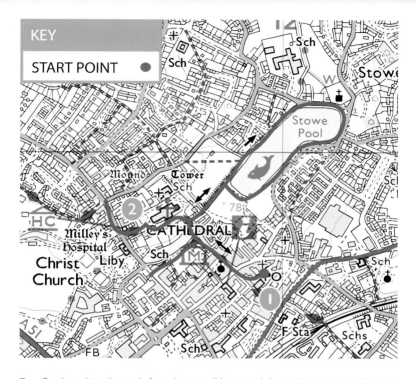

KEY

START POINT ●

7. Continue into the park from here, walking round the perimeter in a clockwise fashion, passing the tennis courts and bowling green and eventually reaching a small stream just before the golf course. Turn right along the side of this then pass a lake with boat hire to eventually reach a bridge on the left, which you should cross. Then follow the footpath from there until you reach Shaw Lane. Continue along it to reach the junction with Beacon Street.

8. Turn right along Beacon Street then take a left turn into The Close. This leads to Lichfield Cathedral. But before you visit that turn left to visit the house of Erasmus Darwin and the herb garden. Then visit the Cathedral. When you have done so, continue past the Cathedral on the right side, where you will pass the Cathedral Coffee House and toilets, then turn right into Dam Street. From here trace your outward route back to the start.

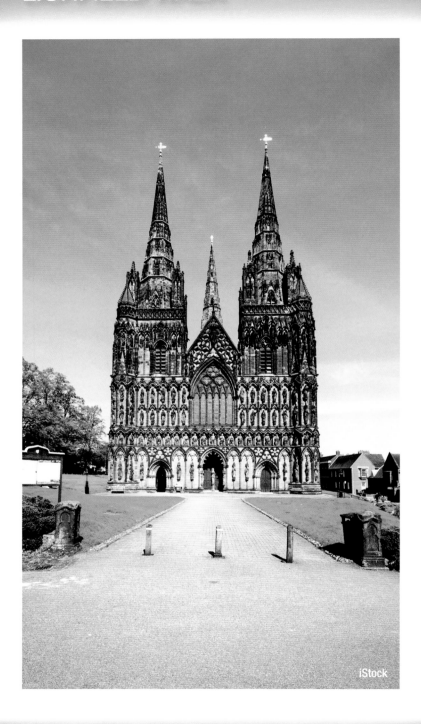

iStock

iStock

ALREWAS

An ideal walk to enjoy the bustle of life on the canal and indulge in a bit of gongoozling.

'Gongoozler' is the term used on canal boats for those who stop to observe the efforts of the boaters as they work their way up or down the locks. It is impossible to walk along a canal without gongoozling, because the whole process is so fascinating. This walk has ample opportunities for it, with locks on the walk and several more at the busy Fradley Junction.

Although canals were constructed by civilisations as long ago as the Egyptians, 6,000 years ago, and the oldest canal still in use was made by the Chinese over 2,000 years ago, the difficulty was always to move boats from one level to another if the start and end of the canal were at different levels, as they usually are. Various solutions were found, such as damming the canal at points and dragging the boats to the next level. Then, just over 2,000 years ago, the Greeks had the idea of putting a gate in the dam so that a flash flood could be created to carry boats down. This was fraught with danger for boats going up against the power of the water, as you will easily realise if you watch how a rising boat is tossed around in a lock. The Chinese designed the first double lock gate around 1,000 years ago.

The lock, an ingenious mechanism to allow boats to move up or down on a canal, is essentially a boat-sized tank at the point in the canal where the level changes. The lock has doors at each end and paddles, which can be opened to let water into or out of the tank. To move up the canal, boaters have to make sure that the water in the lock is at the lower level. If it isn't, they have to use a lock handle on the ratchets on the bottom gates and open the paddles to let water out. When the water is at their level, they close the paddles, open the gates and sail the boat in. They then close the gates and go to the top gate to let more water in until the boat floats up to the top level. Close the paddles, open the gates and the boat sails out, to the appreciation of the gongoozlers.

THE BASICS

Distance: 3 miles / 4.8km

Gradient: Flat

Severity: Easy, when the footpath is cleared. It sometimes gets overgrown

Approx. time to walk: 2 hours

Stiles: Two

Map: OS Explorer 245 (The National Forest)

Path description: Canal towpath, road, field and canalside footpath

Start point: Alrewas, at canal bridge no. 48 (GR SK 166152)

Parking: On road at Alrewas (DE13 7DA)

Dog friendly: Yes, apart from one of the stiles

Public toilets: At Fradley Junction

Nearest food: Pubs and cafés at Fradley Junction and Alrewas

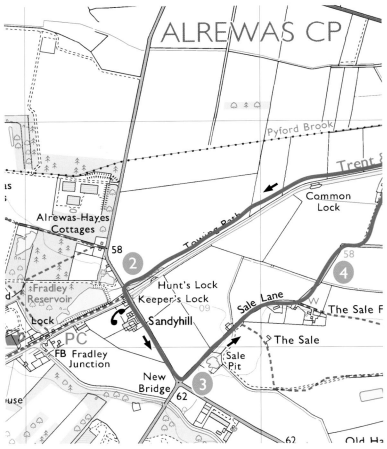

1. From Bridge 48 go down to the towpath and walk along it, heading away from Alrewas. Pass several locks and bridges until you arrive at a signpost for Fradley Junction at Bridge 50. Fradley Junction is a lively canal junction with canalside pubs and cafés and you may wish to linger and do some gongoozling.

2. Cross the bridge and continue on the road, passing some houses on your right. The road is long and straight ahead. At a bend you will reach a junction signposted for Fradley Junction and Alrewas.

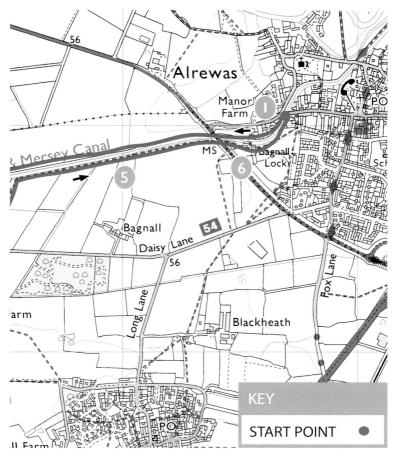

KEY

START POINT ●

3. Turn left towards Alrewas. Follow this road as it winds right and left for about a mile until you come to a dirt farm track on your left with a footpath sign.

4. Go down this track and at a track crossroads before the farm buildings turn right into a field. There is not a clear path here but keep to the left edge of the field and walk right round to the corner diagonally opposite, where you will find a faint track up to the canalside, where there is a footpath marker.

5. Continue along the grassy path between the canal and a hedge, crossing two stiles until you emerge into a field. Go left along the edge of the field, continuing in the same direction to a gate. Go through here onto a quiet road and go under the A513.

6. Continue ahead to reach Bridge 49 beside Bagnall Lock. Cross the bridge and turn right, back along the towpath to the start, at Bridge 48.

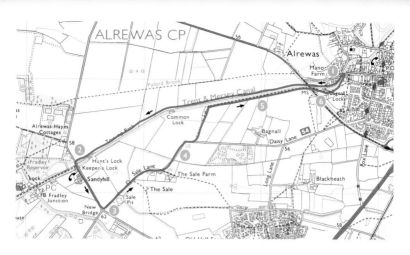

ABOUT THE AUTHORS

Moira McCrossan and Hugh Taylor are a husband and wife writing team now specialising in travel for the over 50's and walking guides. They are also travel editors of the UK's premier over 50's web site laterlife.com.

Moira McCrossan spent most of her working life in education and was a Primary School Head Teacher. An active trade unionist she is a former President of the Educational Institute of Scotland, served on the general council of the Scottish TUC and the executive committee of the Women's National Commission for whom she co-authored the report, Growing up Female in the UK. She was also a frequent contributor to the Times Educational Supplement (Scotland).

Hugh Taylor is an Award winning travel writer, broadcaster and photographer. He worked extensively for BBC Radio, producing several series for Radio 2 including Doomsday in the Afternoon about the music of the Scottish Travellers.

Together they have written or contributed to over forty travel and outdoor guides, some of which have been translated into several languages. They range from major country guides covering Scotland, Lebanon and Jordan to walking books throughout the UK. Their work has appeared worldwide in publications as diverse as The Times, Women's Realm, Choice, The Herald, Interval World and the Glencairn Gazette. They live in the picturesque southern Scottish village of Moniaive and in Capena, a hill town just north of Rome.

The authors would like to thank Rob Ganley and the team at the Press Office of the Camping and Caravanning Club for providing their accommodation and the managers on the Club site at Cannock Chase, Conkers and Moira for local knowledge and advice.